This book is dedicated to my daughters who are my greatest joy and driving force in life. I never knew how powerful love could be until God blessed me with children. For them, I am thankful every single day. -Tina

TABLE OF CONTENTS

FOREWORD

BY REBECCA MERRITT DAVIS

People with Narcissistic Personality Disorder (subsumed in Cluster B the dramatic, emotional, and erratic group of personality disorders) emotionally abuse others in their daily family lives. Their superficial relationships exist to regulate their self-esteem (DSM-V; 2013); they may appear jovial and magnanimous with high self-esteem and vindictive, controlling, and angry in periods of diminished self-esteem. Their emotional abuse is a form of domestic violence affecting the other parent, children, and extended family; institutional settings (e.g. work, school and family court) may be touched by this abuse. Narcissistic parents will harm their children even if they love them because their impaired empathy and hypersensitivity causes them to blame the other parent, to lash out at people they perceive to not be on their side, and to do everything in their power to convince the family court system of their superiority over the other parent. Narcissists vary in their abilities to hide their abusive side in the presence of esteemed others; those with better impression management skills are more successful in court.

Tina Swithin is a dynamic individual with a mission to increase awareness of narcissism and its impact upon shared parenting and divorce among the Judges, CPS workers, Guardians Ad Litem, Parenting Coordinators, and attorneys handling divorce and custody cases in our family court system. Her Facebook group (www.facebook.com/onemomsbattle) is viewed by thousands of people navigating the treacherous courtroom terrain associated with leaving a narcissist and protecting their children from narcissistic rage, gas lighting, and prolonged emotional abuse. This online community is a village of survivors united in problem solving and making positive educational and dynamic changes in the family court system. Tina and her village hope to get court personnel to realize that one disturbed individual can create and maintain high conflict divorce cases inundating the court with years of unnecessary grievances while taxing the economic and psychological resources of the other parent. The demand upon the court's time created by vengeful narcissists could be lessened if court personnel could identify patterns associated with Cluster B personality disorders, recognize the need for psychological evaluation, understand the chronic nature of these behaviors, and take timely steps to protect children and the other parent. It is my fervent hope that Tina's books will make their way into the courtrooms of every family court Judge as well as domestic violence agencies.

Tina developed her expertise and knowledge the hard way – marrying and divorcing a narcissist. I developed my expertise the easy way, years of graduate school, obtaining the Ph.D. in Clinical Psychology, and working as a professor at Purdue University for more than 20 years where I taught doctoral students how to assess, diagnose, and treat individuals with personality disorders. My skill set includes a good understanding of the dynamics driving Cluster B personality disorders. When a family member married and divorced an individual with these dynamics I observed the damage experienced by children when the court is slow to recognize the severity of Cluster B disorders and delay protection of the children. Courts often assume both parties are equally to blame for creating and maintaining a high conflict case, so the non-narcissistic parent is treated as skeptically as the narcissistic parent. This is confusing to the other parent who listens to the narcissist spouting lies in the courtroom and describing self as the most devoted, caring parent. The courts may eventually recognize the need to take action and protect children of narcissistic parents but delayed action results in prolonged emotional abuse during children's crucial developmental years.

Thousands of men and women in the family court system are battling with a narcissist, their children are not being adequately protected, and the court may grant primary custody to the narcissist who is able to glibly lie and manipulate in court. The non-narcissistic parent usually experiences anxiety in court while the narcissist may relish a performance platform to persuade the Judge they are the most worthy parent. Narcissistic parents voluntarily become delinquent in child support (financial control over other parent) will sob in court as they protest their undying love for their children and yet Judges will fail to recognize the discrepancy between courtroom statements and their behaviors outside of the courtroom. When unaffected parents become anxious or depressed from dealing with the narcissist's abusive behaviors, they may be deemed psychologically unstable, placing them at risk of losing custody to the abuser. When their children report abuse by the narcissistic parent, the courts and CPS too frequently conclude that the other parent is alienating the children from the narcissistic parent. It is a challenge of immense proportion to set and maintain appropriate boundaries within the family and within the family court setting with narcissists. This book should be a valuable resource for family court professionals in helping them develop an understanding of narcissism and its impact upon families and the court. For those in the midst of courtroom battles, this book, combined with participation online, will help the other parent increase their coping strategies and skills in dealing with a narcissist in family court, allowing them to move beyond victimization and becoming a parent warrior, a survivor who is capable of protecting her or his children.

American Psychiatric Association (2013). *Diagnostic and Statistical Manual of Mental Disorders* (Fifth Ed.). Arlington, VA: American Psychiatric Publishing. pp. 646–649. ISBN 978-0-89042-555-8.

<u>PREFACE</u>

A young Marine preparing to roll onto the frontlines of the battlefield would not ask his civilian friends for advice on how to ready himself for war. This young marine would turn to a respected military leader or an honored veteran for guidance on how to prepare for battle. Going through a divorce with an individual who has a diagnosed or suspected personality disorder requires solid advice from the men and women who have personally been on the battlefield. A divorce from someone with Narcissistic Personality Disorder (N.P.D.) isn't an ordinary divorce; this is a battle to protect your children, your livelihood, your reputation and many times, your life.

If you have read my first book, *"Divorcing a Narcissist: One Mom's Battle,"* you know about my plight to protect my daughters during a high-conflict divorce that received international attention. My battle began in January of 2009 and ended in July of 2013. While I am not naïve enough to think that my battle is completely over, my children and I currently have peace. In some ways, I feel like I have lost over four years of my life. In other ways, I feel that there was a purpose to my pain. I receive comfort in the fact that my journey has given hope to thousands of people around the world.

In 2008, my therapist said three words that would change the course of my life forever; "narcissistic personality disorder." As quickly as those words left her mouth, I wanted her to take them back. I didn't want to hear that my marriage was irreparable or that my husband couldn't change. I am a fixer. I couldn't comprehend that there was something affecting him that I could not repair. Despite the fact that I was in a lonely, empty and verbally abusive marriage, I wasn't ready to throw in the towel. My daughters were young, only 2 and 4 years old and, in my heart, I needed to know that I had done everything possible to salvage my marriage.

I spent the remainder of that year trying to salvage my wedding vows despite those three little words, "Narcissistic Personality Disorder" that were constantly nagging at me. I was a shell of the person I had been when I first met Seth. I was no longer a bright, bubbly free-spirit. I was insecure and filled with self-doubt. I was in a fog; I no longer recognized the person staring at me in the mirror.

During that year, I began to discover that my marriage was fraught with lies and deception. The man that sat across from me at the dinner table was *not* the man that I thought I had married. The man across the table was involved in financial schemes and had stolen his parent's retirement savings while racking up 1.6 million dollars in debt, much of which was done behind my back. Seth showed zero remorse and seemed incapable of empathy. To those around us, we were the golden couple. However, behind closed doors, my life was a living hell.

Shortly after our marriage therapist recommended a psychiatric evaluation, Seth announced that our relationship was over. A sense of relief washed over me like I had never experienced. That relief was short lived as I quickly discovered that the only one thing worse than being married to a narcissist was divorcing a narcissist.

At the same time, I discovered that the family court system is not educated on individuals with personality disorders, nor are they equipped to deal with them. Narcissists tend to be charming and charismatic. They are also pathological liars who are skilled at deceiving those around them whether it is in the business world, political arena or, sadly, the courtroom. Because perjury is not punishable in family court, this venue becomes a playground for the narcissist and winning becomes their driving force.

With the exception of our final hearing, I personally represented myself in family court for the entire four year saga. In addition to being a full-time, single mother, I acted as my own attorney in a desperate attempt to protect my children. This is a battle that I don't wish on anyone and it is my hope that continuing to speak out will create a ripple effect of change in the courtrooms. My custody battle defied logic by every sense of the word. Over a four year period of time, we endured the following:

- Over thirty court dates consisting of both trials and hearings.

- Two full custody evaluations: Initially in 2010 and again in 2013.

- Six-hundred plus hours devoted to court documents, trial preparation and research.

- Twelve police reports which ranged from Seth breaking into my home to driving the girls without a license.

- Three Child Welfare Investigations which ultimately determined that Seth was a "moderate risk" yet did nothing to protect my children. The following items were investigated:

    1. 2010: Leaving my 2 ½ year old daughter sleeping in a car for 30-45 minutes while he watched a triathlon on television at a gym. She had just been released from the hospital after having a complex seizure and had strict orders never to be left unattended. A court evaluator reported him to child welfare services. They were satisfied when Seth told them that he would never do it again and closed the investigation.

    2. 2012: Leaving both of my daughters unattended in a swimming pool which resulted in a near drowning. My youngest daughter slipped off her "noodle" and went under

water multiple times. My oldest daughter left her own flotation device to save her sister and also went under water multiple times. The girls were 5 and 7 years old at the time. I suspect that Seth had fallen asleep due to a hangover. Child welfare services gave him a pamphlet on the dangers of swimming pools and closed the investigation.

3. 2013: Hitting my daughters and squeezing their arms to the point that my oldest daughter locked herself in a bathroom to escape her father. Afterwards, Seth made her sit down and write all of the positive things that had happened that day. The case was closed because there were no visible marks or bruises.

To Seth, the custody battle was not about his love for our daughters or wanting to be a part of their lives-- it was about winning and, ultimately, his driving force was to hurt and control me. Because he had lost all power and control over me when our marriage ended, the children were his last weapons. Sadly, this is true in most high-conflict custody battles. A narcissist, when compared to the dead-beat parents that the court is accustomed to seeing, is a welcomed relief because they show an interest in being a part of their children's lives. Unfortunately, this portrayed interest is the furthest thing from the truth.

Every day I hear stories from men and women all over the world. Some of the stories tug my heart strings and others leave me feeling shattered to my very core. I've listened as parents discuss their child's bruised or burned bodies and I feel their frustration and their deep-seated pain. I've consoled mothers who mourn the loss of their murdered children and I've heard their despair while discussing the very system that failed them. I hear stories about family court corruption and in other cases, like mine, an overburdened system that lacks the necessary education on high-conflict divorces. The family court system is supposed to act in the best interest of children, yet they are failing miserably. My goal isn't to work against the family court system but to work with them to make changes.

I have spent several years in the trenches and during that time, I have connected with thousands of other warrior moms and dads who share the same battle cry. I walked into this war with the naïve belief that my children would be protected, yet I quickly discovered that in the eyes of the court father's rights and mother's rights supersede the rights of the children. This shouldn't be about father's rights or mother's rights. This is about our children's right to be safe, loved and cared for.

Through my voyage in the family court system, I have learned a great deal. The old adage, "If I knew then what I know now" applies to my custody battle. I learned many things through trial (pun intended) and error. Along the way, I also learned that I am a fierce mama bear and that I *am* my daughters' voice until they are old enough to have a voice of their own. It is my hope that the things I have learned will benefit you in your own battle to protect your own children.

I believe that there is a preconceived notion that it takes two to tango when it comes to high conflict divorce. That is simply not true and this is one of the falsehoods that I hope to correct through my advocacy and outreach. Simply put, divorce triggers abandonment issues in the narcissist and a break-up leaves him void of narcissistic supply. I like to think of this as a heroin addict without his next fix. Addicts will lie, cheat and steal to get their drug and a narcissist will do the same. Narcissists will embark on smear campaigns, fabricate stories and tell blatant lies to paint themselves into the role of the victim. The narcissist will appear to be the parent of the year even if they were never previously involved in the child's life. This is done for the sole purpose of maintaining control over what he views as his possessions: his ex-wife and children. Because individuals with NPD are so charismatic and convincing, the court system often believes them and it can take years to undo the damage.

While it is a daunting and can be incredibly discouraging, it is also imperative to maintain a strong presence in custody evaluations, psychological evaluations and other post-divorce related events. It is a fine line to remain proactive without appearing to be controlling. Choosing your battles wisely and checking in with your inner voice of reason is incredibly important during high conflict divorce. It is also critical to align with a team of people who understand high-conflict divorce and narcissistic personality disorder.

There seems to be a common stereotyping of victims of narcissistic personality disorder. The reality is that everyone is a potential target—not just individuals with low self-esteem. Anyone who can fill the narcissist's personal voids has a bullseye on their soul. Narcissists will target individuals who are loving, caring and empathetic because they are not capable of those traits. Many tend to go after individuals who are successful, career-driven professionals or those who have a strong financial backing because it will benefit them in both status and prestige. I have coached victims from all walks of life – from stay-at-home mothers to accomplished physicians. Known as vampires, they will suck their victims dry in every aspect of life and unless you are educated on the warning signs, no one is immune to these individuals.

In this book, I will share advice and tips for every stage of the narcissistic battle whether you are dating a narcissist, married to a narcissist or fighting to protect your children from a narcissist. In addition to my own advice, I will be sharing advice from the battlefield – from my mentors, friends and followers of my blog, One Mom's Battle. In the first two years of my battle, I felt incredibly alone. At that point in time, there wasn't a single person in my world who understood what I was going through. By offering advice from my comrades in the trenches, I hope that no one else ever feels alone in this battle. This movement is no longer One Mom's Battle. This movement currently boasts over 95 Chapters (OMB Cheer Teams) spread throughout the world. What started as one mom's battle has become a voice and a platform for men and women all over the world.

Wherever you are in this journey, I am sending you prayers, positive thoughts and loads of pixie dust. You will make it through the darkness and the light on the other side is shining brightly. It is my hope that after reading my book, you will feel hopeful, empowered, less alone and ready to reclaim your life.

With love and light, Tina

Though she be but little, she is fierce!"- **William Shakespeare**

DATING A NARCISSIST

I think that in an effort to heal, it is incredibly important to understand why we were initially drawn towards someone with Narcissistic Personality Disorder. For me, this has proven to be a journey of self-discovery filled with honesty, reflection, sadness, laughter and, most importantly, owning my part of the equation. I am not a victim nor do I want to be seen that way.

I was 26 years old when I met Seth at a lake, and within weeks he began to shower me with gifts, flowers, poems, expensive vacations, shopping sprees and affection. I was sold and so were my family and friends. Things moved quickly and while I did see red flags during the first few months, I chose to sweep them under the rug. For a very long time, the percentage of good outweighed the bad. Like I do with everything in life, I chose to focus on the positive aspects of my relationship with Seth, but then I ignored the rest.

Our relationship moved quickly and I was enamored with the life that he was presenting me on a silver platter. Seth's parents had been married for thirty years and seemed to be stable, loving and happy. Growing up in a highly dysfunctional environment, I craved stability and Seth morphed into the Band-Aid that fixed my every wound. He said all the right things and placed me on a pedestal.

Because I had been in a series of bad relationships, I wanted my family to be proud of me and to stop worrying. In the beginning months of my relationship with Seth, things were incredibly good and I could see the sense of relief in my family and friends. When the red flags began to appear, I did not share my concerns with loved ones because I didn't want to face the fact that I had failed – again. I wanted this new life that was being offered to me, so I looked the other way when Seth began to reveal that Prince Charming had a dark side.

What attracted you to the narcissist?

Contrary to what Seth would tell you, I was not attracted to his money. In fact, his bragging was one of the first turn-offs for me. The part of the equation that was attractive was his thoughtfulness. If Seth would have given me a single flower, hand-picked from a garden, I would have been as happy as I was receiving a dozen, long-stemmed red roses. If Seth would have packed a picnic lunch with ham sandwiches, I would have been as happy as I was going to a five-star restaurant for dinner. I was enamored with the fact that he was thoughtful and caring towards me. I had never experienced this before and he promised me a lifetime of this new world which felt so foreign...and so good.

I was also attracted to the stability that Seth promised me. In previous relationships, I was the responsible one. I was the go-getter, and I craved a partnership that was more equal. I was impressed by his drive and his tenacity in the corporate world. He wasn't willing to settle for mediocre and he was the most driven person that I had ever met. He often spoke of all that we could accomplish together with me being so outgoing and social and him being the brains and the driving force.

From a physical standpoint, I was never attracted to Seth. I admitted this to my therapist in the very beginning and she told me that I wasn't attracted to him because I wasn't accustomed to normalcy and "nice guys." He was unlike the "bad boys" that I had previously dated. He was a gentleman who opened doors. He insisted on paying for everything and was offended when I offered to contribute to the dinner bill. Seth made me feel like a princess. In my eyes, he was the most amazing thing that had ever happened to me, despite the fact that I was not attracted to him.

According to Dr. Craig Malkin, clinical psychologist and instructor in psychology at Harvard Medical School, narcissists are experts at "impression management."

> *"Part of what makes narcissists so seductive, especially at the start of a relationship, is that they're experts at impression management. According to research, for example, they're no more physically attractive than the average guy or gal -- maybe a 5 or 6 -- but they've perfected the art of looking like (and acting) like a 10. They can be charming, alluring, and even sensitive (up to a point). Add to all this the fact that, when we're in love with someone, the judgment centers of the brain become eerily quiet, and it's easy to see why narcissists can slip by, red flags and all, and cozy up to us for a good long while.*
>
> *Narcissists who run hot and cold are especially difficult to leave. The ups and downs put you on what psychologists call a variable-ratio reinforcement schedule--the same pattern of occasional reward that keeps gamblers racing back to the slot machines."*

Answers from the Battlefield:

1. In the beginning, he doted all over me; it was all about me. He
    had similar likes and dislikes, the same views on family, the
    future and what was important to me. He made me feel like a
    princess, and that he loved me unconditionally. Once narcissists
    know they have you trapped emotionally, financially and
    physically it's like a switch is flipped and everything is about
    them. They disagree with everything you believe in and you are
    no longer treated like a princess. They convince you that you
    are crazy and you are the reason the relationship is not working.
    They will go to any means to make you feel worthless. Don't
    make the mistake of thinking that they will realize you are
    hurting; they lack empathy and will never understand the
    amount of pain they make you suffer.

2. In my case, falling for a narcissist was a part of my life's cycle.
    I was raised by one, so, naturally, the narcissist made sense to
    me. I was very young, and, seeking to escape the grip of one
    narcissist, I jumped into the arms of another. It took me 19
    years to get out of the first one's (my mother's) grasp and 10
    years to get out of the second's (my ex's). Today, I am fortunate
    to have learned the lessons that cycle taught and I am in a much
    better place to make a healthy life decision in a mate when I
    choose again. Now I know the red flags. I understand the cycle.
    I have seen the ugly side of my familiar. I prefer the beauty that
    healthy has to offer.

3. He promised me the moon, and he seemed to have a plan to get
    it for me. He listened so attentively to all my worries, my fears,
    my reservations.... Then he took those and tried to destroy me
    with them.

4. The narcissist was very attentive and popped up on my instant
    messenger just as soon as I turned on the computer. He was
    there for me at any time. He is still there for me now if I wanted
    to talk, or call him, write him, etc., because he has always been
    that attentive; but the games, control, and the battles are more
    than I ever want to experience again in my life, so I know to

break all contact to stay out of the game and control.

5. The compliments. It wasn't until later that I realized all the praise given to me was in contrast to an insult given to another or, at the very least, a disparaging remark about women in general. "I love how smart you are compared to so many women I meet." "I love how in shape you are. It used to drive me crazy that [first wife] didn't exercise as much as she should have." Classic red flag. No "pure," stand-alone compliment without comparisons and WAY too many of them. Definitely lots of messaging and conditioning going on with those compliments in the early years.

What was it about YOU that attracted the narcissist?

This particular question resulted in a great deal of reflection and contemplation for me. Knowing what I know now, there was an abnormal degree of competition between Seth and his older brother, Robert. I met Seth and Robert at a local lake and there was a lot of alcohol, music, dancing and fun involved. I was carefree and had no responsibilities in life.

From what I've learned about Seth's childhood, he was a quiet introvert who never really fit in. In high school, he was bullied. His older brother Robert was popular in school and with women. Seth didn't date and threw himself into school and excelled in academics. There was a bizarre competition and rivalry between the brothers which took me over four years to see.

Robert's ideal woman was blonde and extremely thin. Seth had an extreme need to gain approval from his brother and his father, Leonard. Because Seth knew that Robert was attracted to me, he had to have me. I believe that I unknowingly became part of a sick, twisted and unspoken competition between two very unstable brothers. I was a possession and I was arm candy. Eventually, I was promoted from arm candy to wearing the title of trophy wife.

From the beginning and in true narcissistic fashion, Seth was attracted to my free spirit and trusting nature. I was carefree and fun. He was socially awkward and boring. He literally fed off of my energy and emotions because he was incapable of his own.

Answers from the Battlefield:

1. The narcissist was attracted to me because I let him lead and be in control, which he loved. As I grew older and wiser, we started to fall apart because I wanted a say in things and I was finding my voice. Now he tries to control with court orders and I can see through his games. A man who wants to do everything and even plans your whole wedding is not sweet. This is controlling. Run!

2. I was a very indecisive person, young and filled with self-doubt. I was still in search of an identity and a clear path in life when I met my ex. This cleared the way for him to take over and guide and shape me into someone he thought I should be. I think part of me wanted someone to come in and take care of me, make some decisions in my best interest and out of love. What really happened, though, was decisions were certainly being made for me, but in his best interest and not mine. Not easy for me to see through until later, when the wheels were already in motion.

3. Looking back, we typically have a nostalgic view of ourselves. We were young, we were beautiful, in the "prime" of our youth. I wasn't looking for the predator that was about to turn my world upside down. Hell, I wasn't even really attracted to him! I am responsible for opening the door. For being nice. Back when my gut instinct still worked, I ignored it. I was friendly. I was empathetic. He must have recognized all the traits my good Irish Catholic parents tried to instill in me. Loyalty. Honesty. Compassion. He must of said to himself, "Hey, these traits look great! I don't have any of these. They will look amazing on me. I must acquire them and show them to the world." So he went about courting me. He was relentless, in a very charming way of course, because that is how they operate. Some of us girls get caught up in the nostalgia of the fairy tale we get bombarded with in this country....and we get swept away in the storm.

4. I think narcissists look for people who shine very brightly. They look for a trophy. They see that as a source of power,

validation for who they think they are. Yet once they have the "prize" they are so threatened by them or so afraid of losing them, that once the "honeymoon is over" think they must destroy them to fulfill and protect their own ego.

5. I believe my childhood experiences molded me into a narcissist's dream. Having a callous, emotionally absent father who was caught up in his own addictions (he eventually left by the time I was 10) set the stage for me to be attracted to a man who was incapable of ever really loving me. After all, aloofness & a lack of affection was the norm, so being with a narcissist merely confirmed the message instilled early in my life that I was insignificant, unlovable, and unworthy of someone who treated me with respect. Consequently I bought myself a ticket for a 30 year roller coaster ride with a narcissist who proved me "right" by lying pathologically, cheating repeatedly, and to my horror living a perverse double life while traveling on his job. The fact that I am a Christian who believes strongly that marriage is a lifetime commitment and that God hates divorce made me the perfect victim, offering a multitude of 'second chances' to someone whose actions inevitably revealed that the only remorse they felt was for having gotten caught. For years I tried desperately to spare my children from having to endure the pain of divorce, but they have suffered permanent emotional wounds at the hands of the one entrusted to love & protect them.

What were the first red flags that YOU chose to ignore?

The vast majority of us had red flags whether they were blatantly obvious at the time or only discovered in hindsight. Looking back, did you realize that your relationship moved at an abnormally fast pace? Perhaps your first red flag was more obvious; such as his mother trying to sneak you out the backdoor to freedom within minutes of meeting you?

For me, there were things I found bothersome from the first few months of the relationship. I take full responsibility for ignoring those red flags. Seth bragged about his dogs, but it was more than just his apparent love for animals. Specifically, Seth bragged about how much attention they generated while on walks. Seth bragged about how much money he made and often put others down in a passive-aggressive manner. Other times, he was very blatant in his disdain for those who didn't measure up to his standards of perfection in every subject ranging from body size to income level and career choices or lack thereof.

There are a lot of other things that I chose to ignore which are common NPD Red Flags:

- Excessive charm: When a person seems too good to be true, he or she probably is! Narcissists are masters at wooing their targets. If you are receiving tickets to your favorite ballet and bouquets of flowers larger than your Christmas tree before the third date, you may be dating a narcissist. Offers to whisk you away to Paris for New Year's Eve are fabulous but could be considered odd behavior if you just met last week.

- Overly confident: A healthy dose of self-esteem is a good thing, but be cautious if he seems to be the president of his own fan club. In short order, you will likely be expected to become the secretary of that fan club.

- Haughty: This was one of the main warning signs that I brushed under the rug. Watch for elitist comments and an attitude of arrogance toward those who are "beneath" him. Narcissists will often put down co-workers, friends and even family members.

- Bragging: Narcissists do not care about your feelings, views or opinions. Narcissists are generally too obsessed about telling you how great they are to even bother asking about you. Their bragging rights carry over to a wide variety of topics including their family, money, cars, physical appearance, elite gym memberships, which college they attended, clothing brands and their career.

- Grandiosity: Narcissists seem to live the phrase, "Go big or go home." They like to be seen and known. Grandiosity is often their middle name. A narcissist will pick up an enormous group dinner tab or buy everyone in the bar a round of shots. Their motivation is to be showy and attract attention. These gestures could be interpreted as kindness, which is the furthest thing from the truth. While a narcissist is signing the tab for dinner, he is simultaneously scanning the group to take inventory on how he can personally use each person whether it is simply to maintain his inflated self-image or for elevation in prestige or status.

- Success: There is a reason why the political and celebrity arenas are brimming over with narcissists. Narcissists are often found in leadership roles where they have free reign to dominate and dazzle those around them. They flourish in big cities where there is less accountability and less risk of developing a reputation that will haunt them.

- The Band-aid: Narcissists are professional Band-aids. They will seek out your weakest points (abandonment issues, self-image issues, etc.) and morph themselves into your savior. Whatever voids you have, they will fill. This sounds great except for the fact that it is short-lived. Once you are hooked on them, they will rip off the Band-aid and leave you bleeding.

- Hypersensitivity: Fluctuations between extreme confidence and extreme insecurity seem to be a common trait with narcissists. They will often imagine non-existent criticism and will respond by shutting down and sulking or acting out in a rage. Any perceived attack or criticism of the narcissist is not dealt with in a healthy, normal way. In his mind, you are either with him or against him and there is no gray area.

- Moving Quickly: Narcissists have a tendency to move at the speed of light. Has he extended an invitation to meet his parents after the second date? Did he have towels monogrammed with your initials as a gift on your first sleepover? This type of behavior is not normal or healthy.

Dr. Craig Malkin, author, clinical psychologist, and Instructor of Psychology for Harvard Medical School, is a person whom I have come to highly respect over the past few years. I reached out to Dr. Malkin for his opinion on how a person could potentially fall for a narcissist. According to Dr. Malkin, narcissists are experts at "impression management."

> "Part of what makes narcissists so seductive, especially at the start
> of a relationship, is that they're experts at impression management.
> According to research, for example, they're no more physically
> attractive than the average guy or gal -- maybe a 5 or 6 -- but
> they've perfected the art of looking like (and acting) like a 10. They
> can be charming, alluring, and even sensitive (up to a point). Add to
> all this the fact that, when we're in love with someone, the judgment
> centers of the brain become eerily quiet, and it's easy to see why
> narcissists can slip by, red flags and all, and cozy up to us for a
> good long while.
>
> Narcissists who run hot and cold are especially difficult to leave.
> The ups and downs put you on what psychologists call a variable-
> ratio reinforcement schedule -- the same pattern of occasional
> reward that keeps gamblers racing back to the slot machines.
>
> One key to spotting a narcissist is to bring your judgment centers
> back online. Pay attention to feedback from friends, for instance.
> They're more apt to see -- and remember -- important red flags that
> you miss, precisely because they're not under the narcissist's spell (I
> call this 'borrowed judgment'). Keep a journal of painful moments,
> and ask yourself, is your partner working with you to understand
> and prevent them? Learn, and watch out for, some of the hallmarks
> of narcissism: Is every mistake he makes, for example, someone
> else fault ('externalizing')? Does she routinely devalue and belittle
> other people in her stories? If so, it's only a matter of time before
> the disdain or indifference comes your way."

In 2013, I did a Huffington Post Live interview with Dr. Malkin and shortly
after, he shared five very important warning signs that you may be dating a
narcissist. The following list is Dr. Malkin's list of warning signs to be aware
of:

- Projected Feelings of Insecurity: I don't mean that narcissists
  see insecurity everywhere. I'm talking about a different kind of
  projection altogether, akin to playing hot potato with a sense of
  smallness and deficiency. Narcissists say and do things, subtle

or obvious, that make you feel less smart, less accomplished, less competent. It's as if they're saying, "I don't want to feel this insecure and small; here, you take the feelings." Picture the boss who questions your methods after their own decision derails an important project, the date who frequently claims not to understand what you've said, even when you've been perfectly clear, or the friend who always damns you with faint praise ("Pretty good job this time!"). Remember the saying: "Don't knock your neighbor's porch light out to make yours shine brighter." Well, the narcissist loves to knock out your lights to seem brighter by comparison.

- Emotion-phobia: Feelings are a natural consequence of being human, and we tend to have lots of them in the course of normal interactions. But the very fact of having a feeling in the presence of another person suggests you can be touched emotionally by friends, family, partners, and even the occasional tragedy or failure. Narcissists abhor feeling influenced in any significant way. It challenges their sense of perfect autonomy; to admit to a feeling of any kind suggests they can be affected by someone or something outside of them. So they often change the subject when feelings come up, especially their own, and as quick as they might be to anger, it's often like pulling teeth to get them to admit that they've reached the boiling point -- even when they're in the midst of the most terrifying tirade.

- A Fragmented Family Story: Narcissism seems to be born of neglect and abuse, both of which are notorious for creating an insecure attachment style. But the very fact that narcissists, for all their posturing, are deeply insecure also gives us an easy way to spot them. Insecurely attached people can't talk coherently about their family and childhood; their early memories are confused, contradictory, and riddled with gaps. Narcissists often give themselves away precisely because their childhood story makes no sense, and the most common myth they carry around is the perfect family story. If your date sings their praises for their exalted family but the reasons for their panegyric seem vague or discursive, look out. The devil is in the details, as they say -- and very likely, that's why you're not hearing them.

- Idol Worship: Another common narcissistic tendency you might be less familiar with is the habit of putting people on pedestals. The logic goes a bit like this: "If I find someone perfect to be close to, maybe some of their perfection will rub off on me, and I'll become perfect by association." The fact that no one can be perfect is usually lost on the idol-worshipping narcissist -- at least until they discover, as they inevitably do, that their idol has clay feet. Stand back once that happens! Few experiences can prepare you for the vitriol of a suddenly disappointed narcissist. Look out for any pressure to conform to an image of perfection, no matter how lovely or magical the compulsive flattery might feel.

- A High Need for Control: For the same reason narcissists often loathe the subject of feelings, they can't stand to be at the mercy of other people's preferences; it reminds them that they aren't invulnerable or completely independent – that they, in fact, might have to *ask* for what they want. Even worse, people may not feel like meeting the request. Rather than express needs or preferences themselves, they often arrange events (and maneuver people) to orchestrate the outcomes they desire. In the extreme form, this can manifest as abusive, controlling behaviors. (Think of the man who berates his wife when dinner isn't ready as soon as he comes home. He lashes out precisely because at that very moment, he's forced to acknowledge that he *depends* on his wife, something he'd rather avoid.) But as with most of these red flags, the efforts at control are often far more subtle than outright abuse. Be on the look-out for anyone who leaves you feeling *nervous* about approaching certain topics or sharing your own preferences. Narcissists have a way of making choices feel off-limits without expressing any anger at all -- a disapproving wince, a last-minute call to preempt the plans, chronic lateness whenever you're in charge of arranging a night together. It's more like a war of attrition on your will than an outright assault on your freedom.

If you suspect that you are dating a narcissist, grab your running shoes and leave quickly. There is no bouquet of flowers, expensive dinner, or trip to Paris that is worth the havoc a narcissist will cause in your life. Unfortunately, it is not easy to end a relationship with a narcissist.

If you are dating and there are no children involved, the most important rule to follow is the "No engagement" rule. Do not call him and do not answer his calls, emails, texts, or faxes. Faxes, you may ask? Yes, there are no limits to the great lengths a scorned narcissist will go to for his next fix. Think of him as a junkie and you are his drug.

Narcissists are not capable of their own emotions so they need your emotions to feed their ego. It could be good emotions or bad emotions – the narcissist does not care. This is called "Narcissistic Supply" and I like to imagine the narcissist in a cage at the zoo with a sign that says, "Do not feed the narcissist." Set boundaries in concrete and stick to them.

If you are planning to leave a narcissist, I encourage you to educate yourself thoroughly on the topic of Narcissistic Personality Disorder. Education will be your lifeline. There are a multitude of online support groups, hundreds of online articles and some great books on the topic. Read everything you can get your hands on. Leaving a narcissist is one of the hardest things you will ever do but it is imperative to your future.

Answers from the Battlefield:

1. On the first night he noticed that I had a lot of books and said, "My brother would really like you." I later learned that one of his greatest sources of insecurity was his older siblings' opinion of him; he felt very inferior. They were highly educated in Ivy League schools and he was the family screw up.

2. Whirlwind romance. On the first month, he whisked me off to Las Vegas and the next month, he took me on a Caribbean cruise. The next month was Valentine's Day and I received a brand new car. He sent flowers often and on our two month anniversary, he moved me in with him. I woke up the day after our wedding to a completely different person; stingy, rude and

demeaning. I dated a prince and married a frog!!!!

3. My first red flag came in the very beginning. After dating a week or so I came home from work and met him on my street. He was already following me and checking up on me.

4. My ex-narcissist asked me for help with a business event. He instructed me to max out his credit card for an important meeting presentation for his company. Weeks later, he yelled and blamed me for maxing out his credit card "with frivolous purchases."

5. Honestly, it was his charm that should have been my red flag. There was so much charm that I remember questioning whether it was real or fake. Between the stories and the constant attention, he never even gave me time to think about anything else but him.

"The first time someone shows you who they are, believe them." -Maya **Angelou**

<u>MARRIED TO A NARCISSIST</u>

Even after being free for 5 years now, I still struggle with how to describe my marriage to Seth. I am known to become anxious and draw blanks when I am asked to describe this disorienting period of my life that lasted for almost eight years. I often equate my marriage to a sadistic boot camp in which I was slowly broken down over a period of time in a very calculated manner. In a normal boot camp environment, the cadet is broken down and then rebuilt stronger than ever. The difference is that the cadet signs up for boot camp as a willing participant. I never signed up to be broken down nor did I ask to be emotionally abused and left as a shell of the person I was prior to marriage.

In my research and while speaking to individuals who have experienced the wrath of a narcissist, I find that the survivors often share similar traits: most are kind, trusting, loving, giving and generally, very golden-hearted people. Those terms have all been used to describe me as a person but they also hold true to the vast majority of people that I meet who are trying to find their way out of the fog associated with narcissistic abuse.

While I never had what would be considered an exceptionally high self-esteem, over the course of my marriage my self-esteem had dwindled at record speed due to subtle and obvious put-downs, criticism and constant and stealth assaults delivered at the hands of the man that I had trusted with my heart. I believe that I stayed in the marriage for so long due to the sheer confusion that I lived in. How could the man who was so quick to write such loving words in cards and poems be so cruel to me? What was I doing to deserve this treatment? If I could just be happier, prettier, skinnier and more loving, I was convinced that he would show his love 100% of the time rather than the percentage which seemed to lessen more and more with each passing year. I felt like I was caught on a hamster wheel and I was growing increasingly exhausted.

My recovery has been made easier by the realization and acceptance of one critical component: Seth never loved me. In fact, he was not capable of loving me. Ever. No matter what I did or what I said, Seth *could never* love me. It had nothing to do with me and everything to do with Seth. I equate this to being married to a robot that was programmed to put on a show for bystanders and shut down behind closed doors. This particular robot was programmed by an incredibly smart, mad scientist who used an un-crackable code. There was no one who could re-program the robot and there was no amount of Botox, self-help books or mileage put in on a treadmill that would make Seth love me. While I believe in hanging on to hope in all situations, there is no hope when you are married to a narcissist. None.

At what point in your marriage did you know something was very wrong?

While I knew that something was wrong long before I said "I do," the first major sign came when Seth bought a brand new cash register during the first year of our marriage. We didn't own a business so I was confused why this unopened box sat partially hidden in our garage. I questioned him about it and he said he would talk to me about it later. He was too busy with work to get into a long conversation at that moment. His reaction seemed suspicious and I became even more curious about the box.

A few weeks went by and I brought it up again. He told me that his company was ripping him off by not paying many of the business expenses that they had originally promised to cover. Since they did agree to reimburse his bridge toll fees during the commute into the city, he was going to print falsified receipts showing that he went into the city daily and sometimes twice per day. The truth was he only went into the city 4-5 days per month, yet he was going to fraudulently create receipts showing that he was there daily. He also planned to create receipts for city parking garages which averaged over $20 per day. I was flabbergasted and speechless.

I left the room while he was in mid-sentence. I couldn't believe what I was hearing. I didn't want to hear anymore. This was a man who was making $80,000 per year. I was floored by how he had justified this deception in his mind and spoke of it as though it was common behavior. He followed me into the kitchen and began to berate me. He told me that if I made more money and contributed more to the expenses he wouldn't have to resort to such drastic measures. This was one of the first times that he successfully turned an issue around and made it my fault. By the end, I was apologizing for being a financial burden and not making more money.

Shortly after that experience, I became determined to find a way to make more money. A conversation between Seth and I months later spurred me to start a new business which had a great deal of financial potential for us. The business quickly took us from an average income to an extravagant lifestyle. Unfortunately, due to Seth's excessive spending habits, we were destined to fail. During the highlights of the business Seth took all of the credit, but during the low times (and there were many!) everything was my fault. It was a financial and emotional rollercoaster ride from hell. That initial cash register purchase was just the precursor to a life of financial lies.

Answers from the Battlefield:

1. I knew something was wrong before we got married. He littered and he thought he was too important to wait in lines at amusement parks. I caught him telling little white lies. I didn't

trust my gut feeling because he promised such a bright future and there was indeed a tender side. There was a broken little boy inside that I felt compassion and love for. I knew something was terribly wrong one month after our wedding when I caught him in a whopper of a lie and he had zero remorse or guilt.

2. When he told me that by getting pregnant I had trapped him...we were already married.

3. There was an undercurrent of anger without provocation. Depression and guilt over a car wreck years before were cited as the reason but never quite fit the situation. Then others started voicing their concerns over the disjointed aggression. I knew something was wrong.

4. The night before our wedding. I had already uncovered that he had lied about things he was doing before the wedding but was naive and brushed it off. Our wedding was in Maine at the beach. We rented a house and both sides were staying in the house. I was preparing for the next day when he out of the blue came up to me screaming that I needed to control my family and just went off on me in a totally insane manner. (My mother was upset because his sister took some food from the fridge that was intended as part of the next day's wedding event. Apparently he felt she should not have had an issue with that and screamed at me instead.) I remember crying on the steps of the house we were renting and wanting to just run away. I felt betrayed. I knew then he would never have my back. We had an 18-month old son together so I went through with it. It was supposed to be a dream wedding and dream vacation but it was one of the worst weeks of my life. I lived through 12 years of that until I got the courage to leave. I did not know, though, that he was narcissistic until I started the divorce proceedings. He was skilled at making me think I was the one with all the problems.

5. I knew something was very wrong when I went into premature labor at six months and he got angry at me because he was

"stuck" sitting in the hospital all day.

How did your spouse handle the pregnancy?

Seth and I had agreed not to have children. We left for a romantic weekend of wine tasting in the Napa Valley with a group of friends. Halfway to Napa, I realized that I forgot my birth control pills. I wasn't overly concerned because I had taken the pill Thursday evening and due to the fact that I had been on the pill for over 12 years, assumed that it would take months to conceive a baby.

One of our friends had brought their 6-month old baby boy and by the end of the afternoon, I proclaimed that I wanted a baby. That statement came after many glasses of wine so I wasn't taken too seriously. Over that weekend, we had sex multiple times and Seth was extremely concerned about the possibility of conception so I agreed to make an appointment on Monday morning to get the "Plan B" birth control prevention pill. I did exactly as instructed and took the pill on Monday afternoon.

Within weeks, I started feeling nauseous. I had a feeling that I was pregnant but was terrified to tell Seth. Once the results were confirmed, Seth took the news worse than I ever imagined. He disappeared on a long run for hours and shut me out for days. I was devastated and scared by his reaction.

Within weeks, my excitement began to grow despite Seth's disconnect. Seth remained distant throughout my pregnancy and seemed annoyed by any mention of morning sickness, aches, pains or even the very first flutters of baby feet kicking. I yearned to have him lay his head on my stomach like I had heard about so many husbands doing. It was a very confusing time because there were moments that he seemed incredibly happy. Looking back, those moments came when people were around to witness his doting husband and father act.

On the day that I went into labor, Seth left me alone and on all fours in a bathtub with intense back labor. He had business transactions to tend to and was annoyed by the previous false alarms. I was nine days overdue and knew the baby was coming that day but he couldn't be bothered to stay with me. He drove me to the hospital upon his return and quickly snapped into his role of the loving husband. My labor lasted 30-hours and resulted in a c-section. I was relieved that he seemed happy with our new baby girl, Piper.

I was released from the hospital four days later and Seth drove us straight to a lake an hour away from our home. A new baby and a wife in pain were not going to stop his triathlon training. Piper lay on my chest in the cab of his truck while Seth swam across the lake and completed his training ritual. I felt that I owed it to him since he had honored my request to sleep on a cot at the hospital for three nights in a row. I was more concerned with how uncomfortable he was than I was with my own pain. Everything was about Seth and any distraction from his spotlight was unacceptable.

My second pregnancy mimicked my first, although it was a planned pregnancy. Seth refused to have an only child and my second daughter, Sarah, came into the world two years and three days after her sister. We had a live-in nanny who was a Godsend to me. In many ways, I thought of her as my co-pilot. Seth was very involved when anyone was watching or when he could brag about the fact that the girls knew sign language at 6 months old. The girls signing at such a young age made them special and more intelligent in his mind. People were enamored with the girls' abilities which fed his need to be exceptional.

After the birth of our second daughter, I moved into the nursery for multiple reasons. Seth was frustrated because he needed his sleep and Sarah kept him awake. The bigger issue was that Seth was disgusted by my body. I weighed 125lbs and in his mind I was morbidly obese. We only had sex one time after the birth of my second daughter and he had to be extremely intoxicated for that to happen. Sarah was two years old when our marriage finally ended. For almost two years, there was zero physical or emotional affection despite my constant pleas to work on our marriage. Inevitably, my requests were met with put downs about my post-pregnancy body, so I gave up completely. To know that my own husband was absolutely disgusted by my body was one of the worst feelings on earth and has left me scarred when it comes to my body image.

Answers from the Battlefield:

1. My wife got pregnant intentionally, mutually, after about 18 months of marriage. Halfway through she did not want to be pregnant, did not want an abortion, kept punching herself. She left me with our son when he was only 18 months old.

2. First, my ex said, "If you want an abortion, I'll support your decision." In a way, it felt like a set-up which gave him something to hold over my head later, but it wasn't that obvious. When I said that I'd never be okay with abortion, the idea grew on him. He started making promises that he obviously couldn't keep. Wanting to become a responsible adult, husband and father were important according to him.

3. Things were actually great up until our wedding night, which is a story in itself. After the wedding, he went right back to his old behavior of going out and partying, and he always kept me in the dark when it came to his whereabouts. Sometimes this went on for a couple days at a time. Sometimes he would leave using my vehicle and would not come home, leaving me having to find ways to work the next morning. I struggled to find a way to get my children places because his car was in the shop for the winter. Five months into my pregnancy, I went into pre-term labor while at work. My doctor told me over the phone to meet him at the emergency room immediately. My husband and I worked at the same company and as we were leaving, he started yelling at me that I should've went on sick leave like he'd told me (he never said any such thing). While on bed rest for the remainder of my pregnancy, he had no regard that my pregnancy was high-risk and his alarming behaviors continued. Our son was born four weeks early and I was to have surgery the following morning. It had been a long day so he went home to get some rest which would allow him to be back at the hospital bright and early for my surgery and so that he could care for our son. He never showed up and the nurse had to take my baby to the nursery. At work, he transferred to the second shift so that one of us was always home to take care of our son. The weekends were his to do what he wanted. I'd decided I couldn't take it anymore. I couldn't bring myself to talk to anyone about what I was going through. We talked about divorce and he said he'd get help. He started attending AA meetings and going to counseling. While attending AA meetings, he met someone and began having an affair. Upon getting caught, he said, "If you tell me we can work things out,

I'll gladly kick her to the curb". I told him to leave. A couple of months later he called and said he just wanted to let me know that he'd had a physical including an STD screening and was clean. I immediately became sick to my stomach and something told me this was a definite red flag. I made an appointment for a complete STD screening and my results came back positive for Herpes. I was completely devastated. I confronted him with my results and he said his was negative and he would show me the paperwork to prove it. He continued to deny giving me an STD but has never showed me the paperwork. He was and continues to be the biggest mistake of my life and I'm not sure if I'll ever fully recover.

4. Mine decided cheating on me 4 months into our pregnancy was the way to 'handle' it. My first born and I almost died during the labor of 47 hours. After giving birth for the second time, he had his mother come all the way across the country to help me transition back into the home after my c-section. The night I came home, she wouldn't move an inch and I ended up cooking dinner for four people while breastfeeding and recovering from major surgery. Strong? No, tolerant and stupid. Now? Free, happy and quite a bit less tolerant. The anger and disrespect from the N curiously intensified during my pregnancy and even while I was in the hospital after the c-section. It has continued to this day, as I still live with him. I never got one speck of caring or concern during a time when I was physically vulnerable and needed extra emotional support. It seemed to make it all worse. I was expecting the opposite. I thought he would see how hard it was being pregnant and it would bring out love and concern in him. It didn't.

5. Nightmare... He didn't believe I was pregnant and made me send him "proof" via hospital records that he then claimed were fabricated. He attended three doctor's appointments even though I was high risk and forty-one years old amongst other risk factors. Hr told me that "being pregnant is not a reason to stop functioning" and would not help with household chores such as taking the trash to the curb. Several times and as early

as three weeks before I delivered, he told me to give my baby up for adoption. He was on his phone the entire time I was in labor. He was then escorted off the floor when I didn't deliver soon enough for him and began screaming, "It's all about YOU!" He was angry that he wasn't able to pick up his older kids for his scheduled weekend visitation. He did not speak to me, hold my hand or anything while I was having the C-section. When we got home, he would care for the baby only when asked and on the second night home threatened to leave and take my son with him. A temporary restraining order was issued and was later dismissed but at least it helped to get him out of my home. He's only seen his son five times in the past five months.

Describe your experience co-parenting with the Narcissist during your marriage?

The first few years of parenthood with Seth were actually the easiest because we had live-in nannies. When Piper was first born in 2005, I moved my office into our house and dropped my position down to 20-hours per week. During that time our nanny took care of the girls and the rest of the time, I was in motherhood heaven.

From the time Piper was born, Seth worked 60-90 hours a week at our business. His spending was out of control and, due to his constant refinancing, our mortgage was over $7,000 per month. I was not going to complain about his absence in the house because we couldn't afford to have him work less hours. He needed to work to keep up with his dream lifestyle. When Seth wasn't working, he was training for triathlons. In all honesty, I found it much easier when Seth was gone because the home environment was less stressful and the mood was lighter. He would come into the house with a dark cloud over his head which immediately caused tension.

When Piper was two years old, she would run and hide when Seth came home from work. It was not the normal, sweet game of hide-and-seek but instead a child who could actually feel the tense environment that accompanied her father wherever he went. Our home would often go from fun, light and playful to uptight and stressful within seconds of his arrival.

In public situations or whenever anyone was watching, Seth and I parented very well together. The girls rode on his shoulders, he was fun and he was present. By this point in time, I had figured out that I was married to two different men. One was loving, sweet and caring and the other was dark, empty and cold. While it was confusing to me, I knew it was even more confusing to our children. In the beginning, I craved public outings because *that* was the husband that I yearned for. By the end, I felt like a fraud and no longer wanted to pretend. I became annoyed and distant after watching Seth's performances and I was becoming more and more distant in our relationship.

Answers from the Battlefield:

1. I felt like a single parent during my marriage. If you asked him he would tell you that he was a hands-on parent and did at least 50% of the work. The reality was that I did it all. Feeding, shopping, clothing, choosing extracurricular activities, doctor's appointments, etc. If we went out to dinner (to the restaurant he chose of course), I was the one schlepping all the stuff and entertaining the kids while we waited for our food. When our food arrived he would frequently be done before I had started eating because I was busy getting the kids set up, cutting food, etc. My ex-husband traveled a lot and I was actually happy when he was gone because things ran more smoothly. Even though he never took a parenting class, read a parenting book or talked to anyone about parenting, he was the expert, and was ready, willing and able to criticize whatever I did while taking credit for the successes. He once told me that he knew the right thing to do because his parents did a good job parenting him and he turned out so well. He rarely showed up to or participated in the kids' activities unless one of his friends was there or he had absolutely nothing else to do.

2. While we were together (never married) he would claim to leave for work every other week for four to six days at a time (which really meant hanging out with his friends, doing drugs, partying, etc). I would take my daughter to work with me during the day and get up with her at night. When he was home, he believed that because of his mere presence and the fact that

we were all under the same roof meant that he was a great father. He would disappear to the gym for hours and spend much of his time on the computer. If we were inside then he would sit outside. He never watched her alone for more than a two hour period of time but when I ended things, he was quick to claim in court that he was the primary caregiver. According to him, I was too busy working, playing soccer, etc to be a mother.

3. The narcissist in my life was a workaholic who also liked to party. So he would come home for supper with the kids (because he was a "family man"), and then go out with his friends. I coached the kids' soccer teams, drove them to swim practice, and volunteered at swim meets. He never showed any interest in helping or attending. When I would invite him to join us, or even when I told him how much it would mean to them, his answer was "I have better things to do with my time." That pretty much summed things up!

4. In my experience, there is no such thing as co-parenting with a narcissist. I was the only parent to our kids...and to HIM. I was the sole caregiver, boo boo kisser, disciplinarian, and playmate. He was always too busy, unless he was "enlightening" them by watching a movie with them of his choosing. When they were sick, I took care of them. When they had appointments, I made the appointments and took off work to get them there. I worked, cooked, cleaned, helped with homework, all while he was the "fun" parent. He undermined everything I did. I'd tuck them in for bed just to find that he had snuck them into the computer room because he "had something to show them" or "wanted to talk to them." I always looked like the bad guy when I made and enforced rules. To make matters worse, he would often lay in bed at night screaming my name (while I was up late preparing dinner for the next night when I got home from work) until I responded. I'd get in there just to have him ask me for a glass of water or to turn the hall light off. It was like having another toddler in the house. After we separated, he made me out to be the bad guy again because I left him. And guess what?

He's still the "fun" parent while I take care of REAL life. It never ends...

5.   Where to start? My ex-narcissist is the charmer and the everyone-loves-him type. I believe in my heart that there are only two people who walk this earth that truly know how he really is...me and his mom. He was very involved, especially when he had an audience. He constantly undermined me in private yet publicly said I wore the pants in the family. Whenever he "announced" this to friends, family and our boys, I remember feeling so confused. I certainly did not feel like I wore the pants and didn't understand why he'd tell people and our boys that I did. In private and in front of the kids, he would respond to my opinions/actions/thoughts in a way that said I was immature, silly, ridiculous, etc. I'll never forget when he said he was worried about his sons marrying a woman like me. He said this to my kids. Again, I was *so* confused because I was a loving, giving, sensitive, caring, supportive, forgiving wife/mom who would do ANYTHING for my boys. He would (and still does) allow the boys to refer to me as "she." During our nightly dinner lectures – given by him of course – he would use me as the example of "how not to behave." Oh my, if people on the outside only knew what it was like behind closed doors. I was under his spell, I didn't even know what was happening as it happened. To say the least, it's been a very difficult 2 years since he left. I am left trying to earn the respect of our boys…and it's a work in progress.

Marital Bliss: The Rollercoaster Ride

My marriage was pure insanity. It was best described as a bipolar relationship on steroids. The highs were amazing and the lows were something that I wouldn't wish on anyone. It's amazing that one could feel as desperate and alone as I did while married. I felt isolated in the fact that we were living a façade. We lived in a pretend world and I was a Stepford wife. How could I reach out and explain the pain that I was in when everyone thought I was married to Prince Charming? The very people that I claimed were my closest friends were not really my friends because they didn't even know who I really was. They only knew the happy wife who smiled despite the pain they didn't see.

We had the home that our friends envied, yet I never fully unpacked my emotions and moved myself into the house because I knew it wasn't real. I knew that our life was fake and that we couldn't really afford that house. I never called it my "home." A home is supposed to feel comforting and loving. I never had a home when I was married to Seth. It was all pretend. I didn't want to play pretend anymore. As each year went by, I was finding it more and more difficult to pretend to love Seth and with each year, he was draining my soul. I was married yet I had never felt so alone in my entire life.

Answers from the Battlefield:

1. Once the wonderful suitor – who was everything I dreamed about – had the ring on my finger, he disappeared. It was all a theater show with drama and control. He controlled my finances, my appearance, my parenting, the way I washed clothes, cleaned house, etc. I, who was faithfully committed to him, was accused of adultery and betrayal (he, of course, was the one doing those things). I was accused of abusing the children (he was physically and emotionally abusing my son who was his stepson). I was accused of being disagreeable, starting arguments, being too emotional and too difficult to get along with when I rightly questioned his abusive behaviors. He had me questioning myself, losing my sense of self. He cut me off from family and friends so he and his narcissistic family were my only "support." Then they systematically and psychologically abused me until there was only a fragment of me left. I did not have the strength to leave but he did me the huge favor of walking out with the kids. I collapsed, cried, begged, and after about 10 days started getting pieces of myself back because I wanted my children. I reached out to family and friends. They helped me heal and get my children back home. I learned about NPD and domestic violence. I fought legally for years and now have full legal and physical custody with his parenting time supervised by third party. He hasn't exercised visitation in nine months and rarely calls. Their attempt to paint me as psychologically ill did not work (he was placed in mental

health hospital against his will by police). Their attempt to portray me as abusive to Child Protective Services multiple times ended up with them being held responsible for brainwashing and emotionally abusing my babies. I no longer care what they say or think about me as I know they are sick, manipulative people who need to be supervised around my children. I found a great therapist for the children, who are happy and thriving. I found a great second husband who has empathy, a conscience, and who loves me and my children. Life is good.

2. He was a child. I was an adult. Wait... He made me feel like I was the child while HE was the adult. Oh no...I'm confused again. I was 19 when we met. He was 28. I guess he WAS the adult. He molded me into what he wanted, we had 2 kids, and 16 years later, I left him...beaten down, afraid, and trying to be strong again. I'm still trying, and succeeding more and more each day.

3. He was like a tsunami, earthquake and tornado all wrapped up into one, thrusting you into his crazy, delusional world. As much as you fight not get sucked into his game, he fights even harder with love bombing, manipulating your time, brain washing, pathological lying, gas lighting and isolating you from your friends/family. Once he has you worn down and hooked, his mask slips and you are in a constant state of anxiety and fear. The only way to survive is for survival mode to kick in to prepare for the emotional roller coaster of craziness. By this point you are unable to think straight to find the door out of the relationship. When you are finally, completely and utterly broken down he discards you for a new victim and his cycle of craziness begins yet again. He never lets go of you or any other past victim because he loves the game of terrorizing each and every one of his victims with his mental games. It is hell on earth.

4. A narcissist is a person who will torment you with both manipulation and abuse. They seem to disgustingly gain pleasure watching you in emotional or physical agony. Right at

your breaking point, he will turn from Hyde into Jekyll behavior and tell you how sorry he was but that you made him do it. It's a never ending "mind fuck" of a roller coaster and it makes you question your own sanity because no one can believe that your partner is capable of such things. He seems like such a great person to outsiders.

5. I went from being a whole and happy person full of life and dreams into someone who accepted that she was crazy, clingy, and delusional. I couldn't even believe the most obvious things in front of my face because I didn't trust myself anymore. My identity was stolen from me in my attempt to be what he wanted me to be. I had longed for him to look at me the way he did at the beginning but in the end, I realized I was just there for "show" and as someone that he kept around as a reflection upon himself. I started to long to go out with him because in public, he treated me like a queen and was so affectionate with me but at home, I was garbage. All my joy, hopes and dreams of a fairy tale life were replaced with this huge, black cavity in my chest full of grief and decay. After mustering up the courage to leave him, I realized I didn't know who I was anymore, and had to find myself all over again. It was years before I learned who I was and countless shopping trips where I couldn't figure out what clothes I liked to wear. I kept having random epiphanies when I realized that things that happened weren't because of me. I will never be the girl he married BUT I am someone new who is stronger and wiser.

Gaslighting

I've always been the happy-go-lucky one who can find the positives in every situation. When I first met Seth, a modern-day Prince Charming, I was bright-eyed, bushy-tailed and ready to grab hold of life with all of my might. Seth was drawn to my carefree attitude and innocent curiosity of the world around me. My spirit captivated him, but not in a healthy way. Seth wanted to suck my spirit dry and rob me of my emotions because he wasn't capable of having feelings of his own.

By year nine of my relationship with Seth, you would never have believed that I once lived a cheery life. Year after year, I lost more and more of who I once was. It was a slow process, but over time I became robotic and empty. I found that my memory, once as sharp as a needle, became undependable and I was, at times, left questioning my own sanity.

When I first read about gaslighting, which is also known as ambient abuse, the past ten years of my life suddenly made complete sense. I had been living one of the most intense and stealthy forms of emotional abuse at the hands of a person who lacked a conscience and empathy. Education soon became the most powerful tool to ever land at my feet. In order to heal, I needed to understand what had happened to me so that I could make sense of it.

According to Dr. Robin Stern, Ph.D., gaslighting is a form of psychological abuse. There is a dance that she refers to as the Gaslight Tango. It summarizes much of my relationship with Seth. In an excerpt from Psychology Today, Dr. Stern describes the Gaslight Tango:

> *"The powerful gaslighter (he has power both because he asserts it and because the gaslightee gives it to him!) engages in an ongoing, systematic knocking down of the other, less powerful person, purposely controlling the relationship by telling the other that there is something wrong with the way she sees the world or there's something wrong with who she is -- and-- the gaslightee, by agreeing with him or allowing his perceptions define hers, over time, loses confidence, feels unsure and experiences a growing shakiness of self. Gradually, the gaslightee begins to question what she thought she knew---and gives up the power to stand in her own reality."*

Gaslighting played a huge part in my marriage; it was a constant. One particularly troublesome year towards the end of our marriage, the roof on our brand new home began to leak after a heavy downpour. It wasn't a small leak. In fact, water was running down our wall in large quantities. I called Seth to let him know what was happening and he snapped at me. *"Damn it, Tina! I told you to remind me to have the gutters cleaned out and you forgot. Do you know how much this is going to cost?!"*

Seth slammed the phone down on me in a fit of rage. Had this happened 8 years before, I would have known beyond a shadow of a doubt that we never had a conversation about gutters and I would have stood up to his ludicrous allegation. By this point in time, I was conditioned to accept the blame. Maybe he did tell me to clean the gutters? My mind was racing and fuzzy. I felt sick to my stomach. I knew that he would never let me forget how I had failed. Again.

By this point in my marriage, I questioned both reality and my own memory. Seth could have told me that the sky was red and I would have probably believed him. Instead of defending myself over the leaking roof, I apologized profusely and made a note on my calendar to have the gutters checked semi-annually. Ironically, we soon discovered that the roof leak had nothing to do with the gutters yet somehow, I still felt like that leak was my fault.

In 2013, I reached out to Sam Vaknin, author of Malignant Self-love - Narcissism Revisited, for his thoughts on gaslighting, or ambient abuse. According to Sam Vaknin, there are five categories of ambient abuse. Many times there is a combination of these components in play by the abuser:

- Inducing Disorientation: The abuser causes the victim to lose faith in her ability to manage and cope with the world and its demands. She no longer trusts her senses, her skills, her strengths, her friends, her family, and the predictability and benevolence of her environment.

  The abuser subverts the target's focus by disagreeing with her way of perceiving the world, her judgment, the facts of her existence, by criticizing her incessantly – and by offering plausible but specious alternatives. By constantly lying, he blurs the line between reality and nightmare.

  By recurrently disapproving of her choices and actions – the abuser shreds the victim's self-confidence and shatters her self-esteem. By reacting disproportionately to the slightest "mistake" – he intimidates her to the point of paralysis.

- Incapacitating: The abuser gradually and surreptitiously takes over functions and chores previously adequately and skillfully performed by the victim. The prey finds herself isolated from the outer world, a hostage to the goodwill – or, more often, ill-will – of her captor. She is crippled by his encroachment and by the inexorable dissolution of her boundaries and ends up totally dependent on her tormentor's whims and desires, plans and stratagems.

- Shared Psychosis: The abuser creates a fantasy world, inhabited by the victim and himself, and besieged by imaginary enemies. He allocates to the abused the role of defending this invented and unreal Universe. She must swear to secrecy, stand by her abuser no matter what, lie, fight, pretend, obfuscate and do whatever else it takes to preserve this oasis of insanity. Her membership in the abuser's "kingdom" is cast as a privilege and a prize. It is not to be taken for granted. She has to work hard to earn her continued affiliation. She is constantly being tested and evaluated. Inevitably, this interminable stress reduces the victim's resistance and her ability to "see straight".

- Abuse of Information: From the first moments of an encounter with another person, the abuser is on the prowl. He collects information. The more he knows about his potential victim, the better able he is to coerce, manipulate, charm, extort or convert it "to the cause." The abuser does not hesitate to misuse the information he gleans, regardless of its intimate nature or the circumstances in which he obtained it. This is a powerful tool in his armory.

- Control by Proxy: If all else fails, the abuser recruits friends, colleagues, mates, family members, the authorities, institutions, neighbors, the media, teachers – in short, third parties – to do his bidding. He uses them to cajole, coerce, threaten, stalk, offer, retreat, tempt, convince, harass, communicate and otherwise manipulate his target. He controls these unaware instruments exactly as he plans to control his ultimate prey. He employs the same mechanisms and devices. And he dumps his props unceremoniously when the job is done.

Victims of gaslighting often find themselves in a fog. Because it is such a stealthy form of abuse it is difficult to explain to others who aren't familiar with NPD. I found that writing my truths was incredibly important to clear the fog and to help me articulate the abuse that was happening. Victims of gaslighting may need to do a Google search to find the color of the sky. Write your truth down: the sky is blue. It sounds bizarre but knowing truth versus the distorted Alice in Wonderland world is incredibly important.

Answers from the Battlefield:

1. My ex-husband is a psychologist. He is a master at making unreal things seem real. There is a clip in Angelina Jolie's movie "The Changeling" where she is admitted to a psych hospital and the intake doctor twists everything she says to make it seem like she is lying and confused. It is an exact replica of my day-to-day life for 25 years. It took 5 years of therapy and separation before I could realize it wasn't me. The sky really was blue, not the orange he had convinced me it was.

2. He told people that I beat him, and I was crazy and stalking him when he was stalking me. When we talked and I would bring up things he said, he would say I was remembering wrong. He said I must have been flashing back to my childhood abuse because he would have never said that. He would purposely do things to yell at me about. He would turn up the heat on the thermostat and then blame me for the high temperatures in the house. He would say that I was crazy and just did not remember doing it! Too many to even remember them all!!

3. It's mentally exhausting; gaslighting is what pushes you to your emotional edge or over. You end up thinking and analyzing way too much about what they said. They will then change what they said over and over to confuse you even more or say, "I didn't say that!" The human brain cannot process this back and forth craziness they dish out to us. Our brains are meant to take in data and analyze it relatively quickly. With gaslighting, your brain gets stuck on one problem then the narc keeps adding more problems (gaslighting) to your brain's problem-solving section. The brain literally gets overloaded and you end up feeling like you are having a breakdown. Our adrenal glands during this time release more and more cortisol and adrenaline

because of the stress. This makes our minds unable to problem-solve. It's a true nightmare. The first time he gaslighted me I had just moved into his house. He said, "If you ever leave me, I will kill you"...I thought OMG I needed to get away from this crazy man! Seconds later I said, "What did you just say?" He said "I didn't say anything" I remember my mind racing and thinking, *"Of course you said something!"* He subconsciously put fear in my mind. I stayed too long because I was so fearful of him. Once I left, my counselor told me he was a narcissist who used hypnosis & trance by gaslighting my subconscious mind. I started reading about the best type of therapy for gaslighting abuse (trauma abuse), and I came across EMDR therapy. This type of therapy is basically hypnosis which is used to reprogram the trauma situation so that it is not so traumatic. It took one session and I was no longer petrified of him. Do I think he can harm me? Yes. I do not live in fear, yet I am cautiously aware. Gaslighting makes your mind get stuck into a non-stop recording thinking pattern versus being fully aware of what is going on in your surroundings and focusing on your life. My ex gaslighted me every day for twelve years.

4. He had me so confused. I seriously thought I was in the beginning stages of Alzheimer's. I would remind him of something – a date, an event, whatever – and he would get this sad, empathic, slightly bemused look on his face, and reply, "No, we talked about that. Don't you remember?" I will remember those words until my dying day. (I learned later that he told other people he was worried about me. He told the admissions officer at my son's school that I "couldn't" work – but meanwhile he was discouraging me from going back to school OR looking for a job). One day, the mail came early at our house. He worked mostly from home, and he LOVED to get the mail – he was like a little boy about it. But on this day, when the mail came he was downtown. So I went out to retrieve it from the mailbox, and was thrilled to see an envelope from the financial services company that handled our retirement account. And when I opened the envelope and looked at the statement, I discovered the money was gone. All of it. The

entire account had been closed only a few weeks prior. (I will always believe the timing of this was a GOD thing.) I called him and I said, "Why did you close the retirement account?" And he said, "But we talked about that; don't you remember?" And in only a few seconds something inside me roared up and I said, "No, we didn't. I would never have said okay to closing the retirement account." (I am older than he is, and he opened that account only at my request a number of years before.) Eventually he said I was right, he was lying; and then claimed he had done this because he had a prescription drug addiction. Unfortunately, when he started outpatient treatment it was simply like a whole new audience opened up for him. There's lots more to the story, but it boils down to more of the same "now you see me, now you don't." For toppers, he claimed to be a sex addict as well. And our son later told me his dad had been teaching him to lie for a couple of years. Deliberately teaching a young child to lie. Unfathomable.

5. I got to the point where I had to keep a journal for my own sanity. I would have to write down verbatim everything I said because he would twist my words. So much so that I started believing him. I shared the journal with our marriage therapist and he was caught. She thought it was a good idea. Funny thing, though, during our divorce pages in my journal were torn out. He blamed it on our kindergarten-aged daughter. Attorneys bought it. I knew better.

The Last Straw

While I wish that I could say it was my choice to end our marriage, it really wasn't. I had been emotionally checked out for over a year however, I went over the edge when I discovered that Seth had conned his younger brother out of almost $100,000. In a joint therapy session, I sat and watched as Seth discussed stealing his parents' retirement and the most recent discovery involving his younger brother. Seth justified his actions, yet claimed to be extremely remorseful. The therapist looked him straight into the eyes and said, "I hear you saying that you are sorry for your actions but I do not feel that you are really sorry."

That moment was a profound turning point for me. For so many years, I had heard loving, poetic words leave his mouth, yet I never felt those words. I read the romantic words that he wrote in cards, yet I yearned to feel those words. It got to the point in our relationship that I dreaded the cards. I told him that I didn't want to hear the words or see the words. I wanted to *feel* the words. For me, it was difficult and painful to accept that a person could blatantly lie and manipulate with words and emotions.

At the closing of the therapy session, our therapist recommended that Seth take a psychiatric evaluation to help us get to the bottom of the issues that we were having. The theft of family money was just the tip of the iceberg. The problems in our relationship ran very deep and we were in crisis.

Seth notified me and the therapist just hours later that our marriage was over. He stated that the relationship was beyond repair and accused me of manipulating the therapist. According to Seth, we were doomed to fail from the beginning with that particular therapist because the therapist was a man who had been successfully wooed by my charms. Ironically, Seth was the one who insisted on a male therapist with a PhD – which is exactly what we had. I was dumbfounded.

Ultimately, Seth throwing in the towel marked the end of our marriage. By that point in time, he had taken a job in the Bay Area and was gone Monday through Friday. We were civil and settled on a nesting agreement which would allow our daughters to remain in their own beds versus being shuffled from home to home.

Because I didn't understand NPD at that point in time, I was naïve to think that a nesting agreement could actually work with high-conflict personality type such as Seth. The arrangement was very short-lived. Within months, I had exclusive use of our home and he was prohibited from entering by court orders which came as a result of his documented anger issues and stalking-type behaviors. Ironically, he broke those court orders within 24 hours of being issued, which was my first real sign that our divorce was going to be anything but peaceful.

Answers from the Battlefield:

1. It was pretty funny actually. He accused me of buying a toilet 'emotionally!' I was gob-smacked. I understand buying a new

dress, jewelry or shoes emotionally but a toilet? I looked at him while he was screaming at me and thought to myself – he's crazy. Turns out I was right.

2. When I woke up the day after our 4th wedding anniversary (during which I was getting the silent treatment for God knows what) and was shocked to realize we had been together for ten years. He was never going to change. I thought about how disappointed my mother would be with me. My mom died when I was 14, so seeking her approval for my life's actions was subconsciously critical to me. I left him that very afternoon when I returned home from work.

3. I left when my 4 year old son started to act like him. I was all for taking the abuse to keep the family unit intact. Coming from a divorced family, I was determined to make it work, but watching my son learning how to be a "man" from a "man" who treated his family and his spouse like dirt made it a pretty easy decision. I KNEW he was cheating and I even overheard him on the phone to his buddy telling him I was stupid and that he couldn't wait to go out of town for work. The funny thing is that NOW that I left him, he thinks I am unfit to care for our son but it was perfectly okay for the first 4 1/2 years while he traveled across the USA for work.

4. I left after a life-altering incident. I had refused to co-sign on a loan for a motorcycle and he pitched a huge tantrum that resulted in a suicide attempt. He spent several days under a Baker Act hold. DCF was involved because the police report mistakenly stated that our child was in his care at the time. They warned me to act fast and protect my child. I hired a divorce attorney while he was detained.

5. When my four year old daughter witnessed a berating session and said, "Why is Daddy so mean to you?" And then marched right up to him said, "Daddy...you are a mean guy...you need lots of time outs!" I figured if she could do it at 4, I could stand up to him at almost 40. She saw black and white even while he tried to paint shades of gray all around her with his words. That

day, I resolved never to allow him to demean me in front of my kids ever again, or to just me for that matter. Sure, he still says all sorts of foul baloney when he has them (we have two and it's been 7 years since that day) but they completely get it. I'm proud of them. I'm proud of myself. Best worst journey of my life! And I, too, found a happily ever after – after ten years of hell. Never give up. Never lose hope.

<u>Divorcing a Narcissist</u>

While I refuse to sugarcoat things and say that everything will be fine, I will say that if you are educated on this battle and are able to maintain your composure, you have a very good chance of successfully protecting your children. I have seen people make a lot of mistakes on this journey. I have also seen the aftermath of these mistakes and the reality is that one wrong turn can have calamitous consequences during a custody battle.

If you are already in this battle and have made mistakes along the way, do NOT give up. I have personally witnessed the most dire situations make a 180 degree turn. I cannot emphasize this enough. I have seen parents who have been without their children for years receive full custody through a variety of unforeseen circumstances. This will most likely be the rollercoaster ride of your life with some of the lowest lows but there is an end in sight. Everyone's ride is different. While mine personally took over four years, I am one of the success stories and I now have peace in all aspects of my life.

In the beginning, I made lots of mistakes. I was often sucked in by the horrendous emails that narcissists are known for and I not only engaged, but I would spend hours defending myself. I got involved in the he-said, she-said paperwork avalanche that is a sure-fire way to overwhelm a Judge. There were many occasions where I did not choose my battles wisely and I found myself involved in the petty fights that muddied the waters. I am thankful for all of the living, breathing angels that appeared on my path to guide me and give me hope. I have learned a lot and helping others is my way of paying it forward.

This hasn't been an easy battle, as those who have followed my journey can attest. During my marriage, my greatest fear was that my daughters would one day feel the way that I felt while married to Seth. I was empty and broken in spirit. I feared that they would be criticized for their caloric intake, athletic abilities and academic achievements. I feared that my children would be slowly and emotionally beaten into submission. Every time my battle felt like it was more than I could handle, I reminded myself of the reasons that I was fighting. My daughters deserved to be safe and happy. I needed to be able to rest my head on my pillow every single night knowing in my heart that I was doing everything in my power to protect my children.

Obviously, there are daunting factors such as courtroom corruption which makes for an uphill battle that I wouldn't wish on my worst enemy. Thankfully, I never had to deal with corruption but I know many who are knee-deep in the sludge of complete courtroom filth. My courtroom experience was far from perfect but the issues that I experienced pertained to a system that was overburdened and, sadly, uneducated on personality disorders.

Advice from the Battlefield:

1. The process of divorcing a narcissist was worse than I could have ever imagined, but I would do it again in a heartbeat knowing how much better life is on the other side. You will never regret leaving. Your only regret, once the dust has begun to settle, will be that you stayed as long as you did.

2. You ARE all those wonderful things they said in the beginning! That is why they chose you. The problem isn't with you; it's with them. A Priest told me "You HAVE fulfilled your vows. God doesn't want us to be unhappy and living in fear." That lifted a huge weight off my shoulders and I was able to proceed like I was on a mission.

3. Walk gently into your future... breathe... cry when needed...be patient with yourself... buy Kleenex... keep your chin up... stay focused on the horizon... stay true to yourself... and just keep walking, remembering that standing still before the next step is still forward movement from where you have come... Life is just one big wave... hang on to that board and ride it!

4. When you realize that you have had to love yourself less in order to love the person you are leaving then you can begin a new chapter in your life of discovery. One where you can build a new sense of self and take baby steps in building a better quality of life for yourself and your children. Also, you will show your children that it's ok to say "no" and have boundaries, and they will thank you in the future.

5. Take excellent care of yourself so you can be the best parent possible for your kids. If possible, start a business so you can have a flexible work schedule. Create the life of your dreams because now you can. Don't let him/her continue to sabotage. Step into your power. Don't be a victim, step into your power. Be your best self. Learn about parallel parenting, do it and do it with love. Encourage your kids to speak their truth. Listen. Don't tell them how to handle their other parent. Trust again. Love life again because it's a choice and you can make that choice.

Leaving with Children:

If I knew then what I know now, I would have educated myself on NPD and I would have thoroughly planned my departure. I am not a huge fan of looking back at the could've, would've or should've scenarios in life. My first mistake was putting my faith in a man who was untrustworthy and unable to be the father that my daughters deserve. My second mistake was not educating myself once the NPD label was attached to Seth. A narcissist's GPS is capable of going in a couple of pre-set directions which become very predictable once you understand the disorder. The first is to win at all costs and the second is, "What is in it for me?"

Obviously, neither one of the narcissist's pre-set directions are in alignment with the Family Court System's founding principal, which is to act in the best interest of the children. Because the court system is ill-prepared and uneducated when it comes to NPD, it is vital that you go into this battle fully educated and prepared.

I highly recommend finding a support group (in person or online) that truly understands the rough waters that a narcissist can create. This battle is one that is difficult for most people to understand because it defies logic on so many levels. Many times, the stunts and actions of a narcissist make as much sense as a person trying to smell the number eight. Connecting with the men and women from my blog, "One Mom's Battle," has been a life-changing experience for me, but one that came two years after my battle had begun.

In 2009, I fled for the women's shelter with pajama-clad children and lacked a plan for what we would do when we left the shelter. I had less than $200 to my name and did not have a job. The girls were just 2 and 4 years old. The car that I was driving had been slated for repossession. By all accounts, one would say that I was up a creek without a paddle. Unfortunately, I would have to agree with that assessment. I would have, could have, and should have, done a lot of things differently but at the time I had no idea of what was unfolding in front of me.

Advice from the Battlefield:

1. I recommend having an emergency bag packed for yourself and the children. Have some available cash and/or financial resources. Consult with the 5 toughest attorneys in your area and have long discussions with each of them. Get yourself and your children into therapy, preferably with a clinical psychologist who has a forensic background. Have options about where you will go if you need to physically escape. Copy every document you can. Sort, sift, and detangle the financial picture so that you know exactly what it looks like and where it is. Document everything. Find a great PI who can help on a whim should you need extra eyes, ears, or hands. Read everything you can about NPD and read daily. Write and journal privately; do not publicly bad mouth the narcissist. Avoid contact. Find a cathartic outlet for your own sanity, like painting or shooting or kickboxing. Do not date or co-mingle,

but rather focus of settling this shit in your life before moving on. Understand the patterns of behavior in your own life that have put you in a situation with the narcissist so as not to repeat those patterns of behavior. Pray and meditate. Dare to imagine a future that is VERY different. Save every dime of money that you can. Live lightly with great personal depth, if that makes sense to you. I could go on for days on this topic because getting up and out of the "Land of the Narcissist" is a daily adventure.

2. My advice would be to educate yourself on how narcissists think and how they operate in a divorce situation. For most narcissists, it's all about the win, and as we've all seen on the One Mom's Battle Facebook page, they frequently use a scorched earth strategy to achieve victory. Facing that reality, especially when there are children, requires a mental strength that most spouses suffering from abuse don't have but will need to develop. I was advised by an attorney to escape when he was not there. I made sure to leave a note saying I was not trying to take the kids away from him and hoped we could work out a schedule for him to see them very soon. This can help avoid any of the accusations that follow about absconding with the children.

3. Be prepared for the simplest of things to end up being extremely complicated with the narcissist. One of the narcissist's best traits is to make mountains out of molehills. Don't become reactive. Be assertive but not aggressive and leave all emotions out of any correspondence and/or dealings (this goes for legal documentation too). Learn to pick your battles and make concessions where necessary, especially in court. Honesty really is the best policy. One of the things that really stuck with me that my lawyer said is this: "It's so much easier to tell the truth because you don't have to remember what lies you've told." My experience dealing with an N-ex is that they build lies upon lies and eventually they're going to slip.

4. Try your best not to involve the children in any legal matters or in issues with the N. This is not to say that you have to lie to

your children about divorce and all it entails. However they don't need to know the ins and outs of it all. When I was going through the divorce process I was honest with my daughter (she was 5 when it started) and I told her that Mummy and Daddy weren't going to be together anymore. That we were waiting for a person to decide who she gets to live with the most, and that no matter what happens, Mummy and Daddy still love her very much. (Just as an example). Try and keep all dealings in writing if you can. Removing the verbal aspect can really help matters at times. If you're preparing to send email correspondence and you feel overwhelmed, sleep on it and revisit it in the morning. If you are going to pen emails, don't enter email addresses into your email 'To' line until you have gone over the email to proofread and remove any emotional responses. Better yet, draft emails in Word or some similar word processing program before copying and pasting into an email so you get your 'tone' and syntax where you want it.

Be prepared for him or her to attempt to brainwash your friends to his or her way of thinking. You really will find out who your true friends are when going through a divorce with an N. If you have access to parenting courses at a low cost then take every opportunity to do any/all that are available. There are some church run courses that are nonreligious and can be very helpful when dealing with separation/divorce and conflict issues with ex spouses. It also shows the court that you're a proactive parent. Always remember the first 72 hours after leaving is the most dangerous. Change every routine such as the gym, book club and the way you drive to routine places..... Never be predictable.

5. My comments are more specific to an abusive relationship. I would recommend establishing a clear exit plan which involves putting money away if you can. Take copies of all important documents, including his, as you may need them later in court. Know how you are going to exit and sort out the parenting plan early. I had to get a restraining order after years of trying to negotiate and tolerating all forms of domestic abuse on both myself and two sons. If possible, have it cover the children.

Four months later, I let myself be talked into an undertaking which essentially removes police powers from the restraining order. This was a terrible mistake, as during that time I lost assets and was subjected to continuous harassment. I then had to get another restraining order, but this time it didn't cover the children. A week later he took my 12 year old home from school and he has not returned for the past eight months. He is now so brainwashed that he has no contact with loved ones, including his older brother, at all. The court believes the father's lies and given the son's age it is unlikely he will return to us. Get counseling for yourself and the children that is specifically domestic violence-related if applicable. This may help your case later. Educate yourself and the children, if they are old enough, on personality disorders. I believe shielding my younger son from his father's mental health issues contributed to the alienation. Appreciate that things will probably get worse before they get better after leaving and watch out for Post-Traumatic Stress Disorder. Remind yourself regularly that you are taking the high road regarding abuse and setting an example for your children. Most importantly, look after yourself first.

Finding an attorney

"Why can't you both just get along for the sake of the children?" Those words are like nails on a chalkboard to anyone who is divorcing someone with Narcissistic Personality Disorder (NPD). While divorce can bring out the worst in a healthy person, a divorce involving someone with NPD is like inviting the devil himself onto the battlefield. The narcissist appears to be charming, charismatic and endearing to those whom he encounters during the legal process, yet outside of the courtroom, he is calculated, manipulative and many times, downright dangerous. The untrained observer may perceive the situation to be about two immature parents who are not capable of putting their children first.

Sadly, many of the untrained observers are the very people who work in the court system such as Judges, commissioners and attorneys. A narcissist is like the modern-day version of Dr. Jekyll and Mr. Hyde. I once tried to explain to the Judge in my own divorce case that I didn't know the man sitting 5 feet to my right. The man sitting next to me in the courtroom was not the same man whom I was attempting to co-parent with. This man claimed to love his children and stated that he wanted to spend time with them however, his actions did not match his words.

Because most courtrooms filter people in and out like cattle, it is imperative that you have an attorney who understands Narcissistic Personality Disorder and will work diligently to protect you and your children in a variety of ways. Having an attorney who understands NPD will ensure a strong parenting plan and court orders with zero room for manipulation or wiggle room. Dealing with an attorney who isn't educated on personality disorders is an extra battle that you will not have the energy to fight. High conflict divorces are difficult enough without the added task of educating your attorney.

While I represented myself in my divorce from 2009 through 2013, I interviewed many attorneys with hopes of finding someone to take my case pro bono. One of the first things that I quickly discovered is that pro bono work is simply unheard of in family law and you have better odds of finding a needle in a haystack. Attorneys know that divorce cases, and especially high conflict divorces, can drag out for years and result in monthly, or weekly, court dates.

I met an attorney named Mr. Morrow in 2010 who really seemed to "get it" but unfortunately, it was before I understood or had a label for what was happening to me. While my therapist had labeled Seth a narcissist, I didn't know that my divorce was a cookie-cutter example taken straight out of the Narcissistic Personality Disorder playbook. When I met with Mr. Morrow, I was suffering from Post-Traumatic Stress Disorder and found myself unable to articulate what was happening. It was emotionally exhausting and, honestly, it was embarrassing to admit that these things were happening to me. I worried that he would think I was as crazy as Seth.

While Mr. Morrow and his wife, who was his paralegal, seemed to believe in me and wanted to help me, they simply couldn't get sucked into the drama of my case. After our first meeting, Mr. Morrow agreed to assist me with my legal paperwork and he offered to meet with me to prepare for each court date. As promised, Mr. Morrow and his wife guided me through the forms and helped me to navigate the Family Court System. Within weeks of discovering that I had a legal team guiding me, Seth began to harass Mr.

Morrow's office to warn him that I would try to sleep with him along with other various and sundry narcissistic ramblings. I was humiliated as Mr. Morrow and his wife had begun to feel like parental figures to me. I felt like Seth was tainting the goodness of these human angels who had tirelessly helped me. Out of embarrassment, I put my tail between my legs and stopped contacting Mr. Morrow's office as I wanted to protect them from the twilight zone that had become my life.

After that experience, I stopped trying to find an attorney and devoted my time to learning the system and the court requirements. I read everything that I could get my hands on and connected with other single mothers who were fighting similar battles. Going into court in pro se was one of the scariest things I've ever done, but even more so during the times that Seth hired counsel to represent him. He would retain an attorney when he was facing serious issues or consequences; however, he was usually dropped by the attorney within months of hiring them. Some attorneys dropped Seth because of failure to pay his legal bills and others, I assume, dropped him because he refuses to follow orders.

In my personal opinion, and based on many articles that I have read, attorneys have a very high rate of Narcissistic Personality Disorder which is why I believe that they have such a difficult time recognizing narcissism in the court room. Attorneys with high levels of narcissism have a hard time seeing the behavior as problematic when the issues so closely represent who they are as people. This is not to say that all attorneys are narcissistic by any means. Along this journey, I have made friends with several attorneys who are bright, shining lights in the Family Court System and they give me hope that there are changes on the horizon.

If I were interviewing a prospective attorney, I would be very straightforward and direct. I would ask them to describe their personal experience working with individuals who either suffer from Narcissistic Personality Disorder or with individuals who have high narcissistic traits. That question offers a lead-in and one can quickly gauge whether or not the attorney knows enough to properly represent you. I would ask for examples of situations or cases that fall into the high conflict category and specifically, how these were handled. Any attorney who seems annoyed or put off by your questions is not the attorney that you want on your side.

Advice from the Battlefield:

1. Ask the prospective attorney the following questions:

- Define a "High Conflict" divorce.

- Have you discovered a link between the HCD (High Conflict Divorce) and personality disorders?

- Have you ever won a case arguing "Emotional/Psychological Abuse"?

- Define Narcissistic Personality Disorder.

- Do you work closely with psychologists/therapists and/or evaluators who are experienced in NPD?

2. The biggest issue is finding out which attorneys you should interview, but once you are at that point ask, "What are your views about high conflict divorces?" Listen to how they respond and if they assume the conflict is shared, ask, "Under what circumstances are both parties not equally responsible for a high conflict divorce?" At this point you should know whether it is worth sticking around for more questions. My next one: "How are you able to help the Judge realize that psychopathology and intentional behavior in one party can be solely responsible for maintaining high conflict divorce?"

3. Ask around first, and use word of mouth recommendations. I was lucky as I used the law firm I used to work for many years ago. I knew their family lawyers were worth their salt. I was given one attorney temporarily before I got the one that saw my case through.
The temporary one seemed to be less organized and ended up going away on holidays when my first hearing was due. I didn't like how she seemed dismissive of my case and spoke to a partner of the firm who in turn recommended the woman who took over my case. She was very thorough. I explained to her what I wanted and what the situation was and she attacked it head on. She in turn recommended my barrister who was also very proactive. Don't settle for someone who is dismissive of you and doesn't take the time to view the full picture.

4. Ask around for recommendations and the referring party to qualify

their recommendation. Get a lawyer who's quick out of the gate. Find someone who enjoys litigation and has been in the field for many years. Find someone who'll advise you with the truth, not what you want to hear. I had a list of questions to ask my lawyer when we first met. I asked mine point blank if she'd come up against a narcissist before. I knew from her answer she certainly had. I had a very nice "everyone get along" mediator-style lawyer at first and although I liked her, she fell down quickly in court. Your lawyer is your voice. Don't settle for just anyone.

5. At the beginning of my divorce, my ex-husband consulted with the top attorneys in our county which left me unable to find decent representation. Even though he didn't actually hire them, it was a conflict of interest and it was difficult to find someone to represent me. This is a common (and dirty) trick that everyone should be aware of when starting this process. I was left with the bottom feeder attorneys to choose from and to date, I have been through five attorneys. First, I would ensure that your attorney is familiar with the Judge assigned to your case and I would directly ask him/her what other local attorneys would say about them from a professional standpoint. Ask around, read Yelp reviews on local law firms and, if you have the opportunity, sit in the courtroom to which you are assigned. Watch different attorneys and critique how they present in the courtroom and whether or not they have a good rapport with the actual Judge. When you've narrowed down your selection, ask them point-blank to describe Narcissistic Personality Disorder and furthermore, how it relates to high conflict divorces. In my opinion, this is one of the most critical topics when starting the divorce process with a narcissist. The decision that you make on your attorney could make or break your case. You are choosing an advocate to represent the best interest of your children. Choose wisely.

Going Pro Se

Obviously, this is not the first choice. However, it is a harsh reality for many people, myself included. During the course of my marriage, I was accustomed to beginning my week with a professional massage at the local day spa on Monday mornings and driving multiple luxury vehicles. I had live-in nannies and vacations on a regular basis. After I left Seth, my financial status plummeted to the point that I was thrilled to be making

$1,000 per month because that meant I didn't have to beg Seth for gas money or groceries.

While my income has increased to the point that I am no longer living below the poverty level, I've never been in a position to scrape together an extra $3,000 to put towards a retainer for legal counsel. The girls and I have everything we need to be comfortable in life, however, I do not have a savings account nor do I have the resources to obtain an attorney. I have heard of divorces that cost $20,000 in legal fees and I have heard of extreme cases that have cost upwards of $2,000,000. I didn't have $3,000 let alone $20,000. For that reason, hiring an attorney was never an option for me.

To say that I was green when I first started the divorce process would be the understatement of the decade. It took me two painful court dates to even figure out how to *ask* for child support. I resembled a deer in headlights when it came to conflict of any type and a courtroom is the quintessential definition of conflict. To make matters worse, I was not familiar with the person being described in court documents and was left dazed and confused every single time I walked out of the courthouse.

While Seth was using my name, he could not possibly be referring to me. The person that Seth described was an alcoholic. I drank an average of two glasses of wine with dinner during the course of our marriage aside from the fun nights out pre-children. The person that Seth described was completely hands-off when it came to our children, leaving him to do everything. I had exceeded in the role of primary caregiver and was one of the most hands-on mothers that I knew. The person that Seth described was a floozy who slept with a new man every weekend. To date, I had been with less than five people in my life. I was in a fog and completely disoriented for the first three months of my battle. I slowly came to realize that I needed to pull up my big girl panties because my children's lives were at stake.

The local resources that I personally utilized:

- Local Courthouse: My court house and many others offer the services of a "Family Court Facilitator" who will guide individuals in pro se. I spent a lot of time working with our local facilitator in the beginning months.

- Local Law Hotline: I was directed to several attorneys who met with me for a free consultation. One attorney felt compelled to help me with my paperwork free of charge yet they were not in a position to actually represent me pro bono. I was grateful for the assistance with paperwork and this particular attorney even consulted with me prior to court dates to coach me on what to do and what to say.

- Women's Community Center: My local center offers a divorce workshop one night per month to assist litigants who were self-represented with paperwork and direction. Attorneys in the area volunteer their time to meet with each person for a 30-minute consultation in exchange for a $40 donation. The donation was suggested only and not required if the litigant was financially unable to afford the fee.

- Church or Congregation: Check with your local church to see if they have members who are able to offer low-cost advice or assistance with your legal battle.

- Women's Shelter: At the time my marriage ended, my local women's shelter had an attorney on staff who assisted me with paperwork free of charge. Due to budget cuts, they no longer offer this service but many shelters still keep paralegals on staff for litigants in pro se.

The most common question that I receive is: "I can no longer afford my attorney and will be going to court in pro se. What advice do you have?" This is a really tough question for me to answer. I generally want to reach through the computer and offer up a huge hug because I know the fear so well. It's a very difficult question because every court room is different – different Judge, different rules and different requirements. Some courtrooms are more friendly to those in pro se (smaller towns generally) and some are the opposite.

Many times, there is no rhyme or reason to the decisions that are made in Family Court. I often wonder if the Judge goes into chambers to flip a coin in a frustrated effort to find a solution. I have heard of some people walking into the courtroom ready to throw in the towel yet they leave the courtroom feeling victorious. It is impossible for anyone to predict the outcome of a case because there are so many variables.

I can offer these pieces of advice that have worked for me over the years:

- **Courtroom Preparation**: Familiarize yourself with the Judge or Commissioner who is presiding over your case. Spend a day sitting in the courtroom and pay special attention to the procedures and strategies used by attorneys. Many times, you will discover the Judge's likes and dislikes and the experience will help you to mentally prepare for when it is your turn to walk into the courtroom.

- **Bystanders**: Prepare yourself for the fact that the individuals who hold vital information will not want to get involved. To me, it defied logic because these people held information that could protect my children. Ironically, the people who should not be involved are quick to jump in and offer their "expert" advice to the court. If someone holds critical information that could help your case, a subpoena is always an option, which takes the decision to talk out of their hands.

- **Character Statements**: As early as possible, start to collect declarations from people in your community who can attest to your character and parenting. In the beginning, I hesitated to ask people for fear of putting them in an awkward position. I have discovered that the vast majority of people are willing to help if you are clear with them about what you need. Asking people to focus on specific events that they may have witnessed or giving examples to back up their statements about your parenting is important. I suggest obtaining a wide variety of declarations from people who know you such as teachers, pediatricians, PTA members, neighbors and other such community members.

- **Documentation**: I cannot emphasize enough the importance of documenting everything. No matter how insignificant it seems at the time, jot down everything that you feel is out of the ordinary. I personally kept a daily calendar-style journal which allowed me to make quick notations. Sometimes, you are able to catch patterns of behavior this way before you even realize there is a problem. For more significant occurrences, I recommend starting a Gmail account specifically for communicating with your ex and documenting items of concern. I would often sit down at the end of the day and send myself an email to and from this designated account with subject lines like, "Documentation: No show for visit on December 18, 2013" or "Documentation: CWS report filed by school on January 23, 2014." Gmail or similar programs provide easy search access along with a user-friendly platform.

- **Organization**: No matter where you are in the process, organization is critical and will allow you to stay sharp, focused and more confident ,which is incredibly important. I personally use a binder system (chronological order) with a new binder for each year. Given that I was in court 13 times in 2012 alone, my binders are rather large in size.

- **Understanding Court Documents**: Each courthouse is different and the forms and requirements differ from state to state and county to county. It was crucial for me to know and understand the rules for my particular county. I kept a small binder of sample court documents with post-it notes detailing the instructions for each form such as the number of copies needed, dates of service, requirements of service and anything else noteworthy.

- **In Court**: Remain composed and focused while reserving your emotions for outside of the courtroom. As difficult as that may be, it is incredibly important. Do whatever you need to do to stay in the game mentally. Many of the women from my online support group, One Mom's Battle (OMB) write a reminder on the inside of their wrist such as, "OMB Warrior" or, "Survivor, not a Victim." I personally carry a small assortment of items to help me stay centered, such as a photo of my daughters, a photo of my grandfather to remind me that he is watching over me and other personal mementos. Having a friend attend court is also another form of emotional support that has always been a welcomed relief to me.

- **Outside of Court**: In my experience, abusers are quick to use claims of alienation and, in a parent's attempt to protect their child from abuse, actions can often be misconstrued as parental alienation. This was the situation in my custody battle. Seth began to cite parental alienation from the very beginning and didn't stop until the bitter end. Do not, under any circumstances, speak poorly about your ex to your child. Your goal is to protect your child from this battle and your child's job is simple: to be a child. My daughters have been through a lot but I tried my hardest to shelter them as much as possible from the rigors of this nightmare. When the girls would tell me that their father said "not-so-kind" things about me, I reassured them that I was strong and unbothered by their father's words. Worrying about my feelings was the last thing that I wanted them to do. I never veered off the high road as tempting as it was on multiple occasions.

- **Defending Yourself**: Respond to false allegations calmly with credible, factual information but do not get caught up defending every minor allegation, as tempting as it may be. This is the time to choose your battles wisely. It is very easy to get upset while listening to testimony of a narcissist due to the dishonesty and manipulations. Listen calmly and take notes. Make bullet points of items that you would like to address but do not allow yourself to get sidetracked and angered. Stay focused and stay centered at all times.

- **Reminder:** As silly as it may sound, you need to remind yourself that you are dealing with a narcissist. In my first book, "Divorcing a Narcissist: One Mom's Battle," I recommended carrying a post-it note into court that says, "Reminder: I am dealing with a narcissist" simply because many battles in history were lost due to the element of surprise.

Narcissists operate by their own playbooks. They do not follow the law nor do they abide by rules or protocol of any kind. Prepare yourself for blatant lies, vicious attacks, bizarre behavior, and the things that you would never fathom. Your best strategy is to stay two steps ahead at all times, and to expect the unexpected at all times. Another important component to going to battle against a narcissist is to know your truths. Your truth is your foundation and we all know how important a foundation is to a house. Ensure that you are truthful in all that you do and, equally important, know your truths and do not be swayed or rocked by the lies of a narcissist. I am a firm believer that even the believers will eventually see through them.

Advice from the Battlefield:

1. My experience was this: when we were both pro se, the Judge seemed to listen to us both and, rightfully so, ruled in my favor. The narcissist didn't like that so he hired an overpriced goon and got the ruling overturned. I ALMOST had to pay for his appeal but he was six months behind in child support so I was able to escape that one.

2. Stay organized and be calm. The night before I always soak in a scented bubble bath and play relaxing music. I try to get enough sleep. Go over everything with a friend. Write your motion in an easy-to-read list numbered one through whatever. Organize your evidence for each numbered item. Ask the Judge or hearing officer for patience with your presentation. Most important, be calm and thorough.

3. Pro se only worked as long as we were both pro se. The Judge made a clear effort to help us both and listen to us both. As soon as he had a lawyer, I was clearly out-battled. Despite this my best advice is to look at examples of pre-written documents and copy them and fill in for your own case. (As mothers with lawyers, please make an effort to write a blog and make your court papers available for moms who cannot afford a lawyer – it will serve to help those write successful documents and help get their kids back, just black out the names.) Ask the court help desk for advice. Call up the women's shelters and talk to their counselors. I also joined a Yahoo group called, "Non-Custodial Mothers Breaking the Silence." These moms have a lot of legal experience between them. Try to book your case early in the morning, or early in the afternoon. Don't let your Judge try to get rid of you for lunch. I always stay before and

after my case is called. Plan the whole day to watch how he rules. Get to know your Judge on the internet. Often you can find articles or reviews on Judges. If you have not had any rulings you can make a one-time switch. If they have a bad report card, get rid of them. If you have to keep them, find out what they like. If they are a stickler for documents or hate gossip, then you will see it in their rulings. Always dress professionally and act robotically. Be the lawyer you want to have. I bought a suit, I got a manicure, etc. It will help your Judge to treat you like counsel.

4. A lot of time people bring evidence that Judges refuse to look at. Write clear non-emotional declarations and reference exhibits A, B, C and so on and make the evidence part of the declaration. If your ex is violating orders, write "John Doe is in violation of the court order XYZ and attached in exhibit ABC is the proof." Stay away from he said/she said because that is all hearsay and will get thrown out.

5. I finally got the Judge to actually READ my paperwork. I was completely mad and sick of writing briefs and when I confronted the Judge, he admitted he didn't read something or remember the details. That's how I got Judicial Performance's attention. I got several transcripts where he would state this and blatant lies on the laws. The Judge's cannons (rules Judges are supposed to live by) include being ready & proficient in the law. I finally got pissed as my ex-N was trying to take my visitation away. I stood up in front of the entire court and stated this: "Your Honor do you see this seal on this paperwork?" He said to get to my point. I said, "You are supposed to know your cases you preside on, yet you let (my ex-husband) run YOUR courtroom. You misquote laws that are incorrect and I have them in transcript. This is your notice because you choose to not read my briefs and you allow (the narcissist) to act unlawfully. You are now under investigation for being derelict in your oath." The bailiff had to turn his back – he was laughing. He later he told me he's never seen someone do something like that. I wouldn't advise others to do it but I've

been in jail with no charges due to my ex's lies and I didn't find jail bad at all. I was ready for anything. I was not going to let the ex lie and ruin my Christmas yet again…and create another anxiety attack for my daughter. Long story short, the Judge took 3 days to read all my filings (I have an insider in the court house) and he was VERY careful, even ordering an attorney for our daughter which was paid for by the court. These Judges get on a one-way track and stay on it because they don't want to be wrong. Sometimes you have to do something drastic that will get their attention…. Some people will say it's stupid, crazy, rude. Who cares!?! I still have my daughter and now the Judge is reading the paperwork because he knows it may hurt his bottom line….. And Christmas with my daughter was awesome…. And the liar did not achieve his agenda, which was intentional infliction of emotional distress and messing with my holidays and our daughter!

Tactical Moves

Learning the tactical moves of a narcissist is critical to maintaining your composure and winning this battle. While I use the term "winning" several times throughout this book, I want to be clear in my intention. The narcissist wants to win at all costs *despite* the damage to the children. My definition of winning as it pertains to this battle is with the *goal* of protecting the children at all costs.

No one goes into battle without understanding the intricacies of their opponent. Knowing your opponent and predicting his next move also removes the element of surprise that the narcissist often uses to weaken their enemy. While you may be the kindest person in the world who wants to avoid conflict at all costs, the narcissist has declared war and, whether you like it or not, you are now the enemy.

As I come up on the fifth anniversary of this custody battle, I often say that nothing could surprise me anymore. Through my blog, I've either heard it all or experienced it all. In this war, it is important to choose your battles wisely. There are things that a narcissist will do to annoy you and then there are things that he will do to completely unnerve you. Knowing what to document and what to ignore is critical because if you allow yourself to get caught up in every poke or prod from the narcissist, you will become overwhelmed in short order.

Some common things that narcissists will do to poke and prod during a divorce:

- **Misspelled Name**: You've been married for 23 years and, obviously, your husband knows how to spell your name. While it is very difficult to misspell a name such as "Lisa," he suddenly begins to reference you as "Leesa" in emails. The narcissist may also start calling you by your maiden name or he may call you by the birth name that he knows you dislike. Why does he do this? Because he is trying to push your buttons. He is attempting to show you that you are so insignificant to him that he doesn't even remember how to spell your name. Do not point this out or correct the misspelling. This is the reaction that he wants and expects from you. Do not give him the satisfaction of acknowledging his spelling error.

- **Karma**: Narcissists like to remind their victims of Karma. Seth's favorite line in person, by phone, through emails and while shouting from the rooftops was that "Karma is going to get you." Maybe narcissists have a secret fear of Karma and they project this insecurity onto their targets. Over time, Seth's Karma threats became humorous because I became more grounded in my truth. I knew I was a good person and I knew Seth wasn't. I stopped worrying about these threats from Seth and sat ready to accept my Karma with open arms. I am happy to report back that Karma did get me and I am enjoying nothing but peace and happiness.

- **Verbal Attacks**: Insinuations of bad parenting are rampant and simple issues such as mismatched socks on your five-year-old suddenly become an invitation for an attack. Our youngest daughter, Sarah, was suffering from febrile seizures brought on by fevers. After an exceptionally nerve-wracking seizure which resulted in hospitalization, Seth sent me an email stating that he was concerned that our daughter only had seizures while in my care. I was in shock as I read his email and the mother in me, still shaken from the intense seizure, allowed his words to crush me. Once I regained my composure, I was able to remind myself that I was dealing with a monster. I was able to think logically: of course the seizures happened while in my care. I had 80% custody and Seth left the girls with me whenever they were ill. Over time, I was able to laugh off his absurd attacks, but that took time and on-going education on Narcissistic Personality Disorder. Another thing that narcissists seem to do is bold and capitalize things such as "MY daughter" or "MY son." Can we say, "possessions?" Very sad.

- **High and Mighty**: Narcissists love to feel superior and thrive on pointing out the errors and faults of others. In the beginning of our divorce, Seth would point out my misspellings or grammatical errors at the bottom of each email. It was very pointed and condescending, and I knew how much pleasure it brought him. At that time, he loved to point out that I didn't have a college education and would inform me that he would never allow his daughters to be raised by a "country bumpkin without a college degree." Seth derived a sick pleasure in reminding me of my humble upbringing and the small studio apartment that I lived in when he first met me. While Seth's attempts to stir me worked in the beginning, I slowly took my power back. Ironically, as our custody battle progressed and Seth's mental state declined as a result of stress and alcohol consumption, his emails were filled with misspellings and grammatical errors.

- **Shock and Awe**: Seth was an alcoholic so, therefore, I was a raging alcoholic in all of the court documents that he submitted. Seth was trying to have sex with anyone who would give him five seconds of their time so, therefore, I became the town prostitute who turned tricks after dropping the children off at school. In the beginning, I felt compelled to respond to each and every accusation regardless of how bizarre and farfetched the allegation was. I was shell shocked at the mere accusations and couldn't believe that he actually thought these things about me. I quickly learned that I needed to pull myself together and stand firm in my truth. I was not an alcoholic prostitute and, therefore, I would not waste five seconds defending myself over these absurd allegations.

- **Email Assaults**: You have two choices when it comes to reading the emails from a narcissist. You can become a sponge and absorb every word, attack and manipulation or you can apply a coat of Teflon to your psyche and let the narcissistic psycho-babble slide right off. While you may be thinking that it is easier said than done, you will eventually get to the point where you will actually laugh at their childish attempts to hurt you. Later in the book we will re-visit the patent pending Narc Decoder which will allow you to understand the language of the narcissist. While narcissists once had us convinced that they were special and unique creatures, I will be the first one to disprove this theory. They are all the same. Boring. Next.

Advice from the Battlefield:

1. I had to learn boundaries. It wasn't easy for me but I initially put up some physical boundaries. Like he can't come into my home. No face to face communication; just emails for documentation. The emotional boundaries took a lot longer to enforce, but with time it gets easier and easier to see how pathetic his actions are and to not let them get to me. My therapist had me visualize him on a game board trying to get me to play. The actual visualization of me physically leaving the game board and watching him play with himself was very helpful. Not to mention hysterically funny!

2. For name misspelling, I ignore it. It was meant to push a button but it changes nothing about how my name is spelled. For Karma references? I've adopted a "C'mon Karma" attitude. I could use the break! The condescension seems to be a reflection of how he thinks of himself, not a reflection of what I deserve, so I blow it off.

3. Ignore, ignore, ignore! When my ex found out that I started college, he began correcting my grammar and spelling in my

emails, with comments that I was not ready for college. I laughed at the fact that he was seething at the mere thought of me spreading my wings without him. They are very sick people and I refuse to play the game because they change the rules which allows them to win – in their minds.

4. Take them back to court and request that greater boundaries be drawn including limiting contact but, more importantly, include a clause against disparaging comments. You can even suggest that foul language, name calling, etc are considered a violation. There are a myriad of writings from counselors that substantiate that this type of behavior IS domestic abuse.

5. I found Our Family Wizard (OFW) through Tina's blog, "One Mom's Battle," and it has saved my sanity. I received a court order that all non-emergency communication is limited to OFW. My therapist and my son's GAL both have access to our communication and I finally have peace. Like most narcissists, mine hates being controlled and sent me multiple non-emergency text messages, which caused the Judge to tighten the communication even further. Now, he is only able to send one weekly email on Monday mornings before 10am and I am afforded 72 hours to respond. Since this order was put into place, things are so quiet that I can hear angels singing.

Courtroom Anxiety

As we've discussed, narcissists are the masters of projection and this is played out heavily in court. The courtroom becomes a stage for the attention-seeking narcissist. I had a very difficult time in the courtroom as anxiety took hold and my mind was spinning with the fear of whether or not the court would believe Seth and his lies. I had a very difficult time wrapping my mind around the fact that someone behind a bench could decide the fate of my children with a glimpse into 1% of our world. This concept defied logic as much as Seth's actions through the divorce proceedings.

There were times when I felt very confident and I would march in holding God's hand but there were times when I had to remind myself to breathe. There were other times when friends would have to remind me to breathe because that simple task felt overwhelming. It was very difficult not having family in California to accompany me to court dates and I was too embarrassed to ask friends to attend during the majority of the hearings.

Everyone advised me to check my emotions at the door however, I discovered that it was much easier said than done. Being a sensitive person by nature, I struggled with compartmentalizing my feelings. All of the emotions leading up to court dates compiled with late night paperwork sessions seemed to build with every step toward the courthouse. I've literally found myself in the courthouse bathrooms dry heaving minutes before the door to the courtroom opened.

In order to prepare myself, I would take a rest day three days prior to court in an effort to let go of the stress. This wasn't always realistic but I made sure that I found at least a few hours to clear my mind, pray heavily and re-center myself. I would spend the two days prior to court reviewing paperwork and I would pretend it was a work project or that I was assisting a friend with her case which allowed me to emotionally check out. I would prepare a master list of bullet points based on the paperwork, in order of importance, which would allow me to stay focused on the most important aspects of the case and prevent me from getting side-tracked. I would also bring a small bag of trinkets such as a note of support from my Aunt, an old pearl necklace that belonged to my mom, a picture of the girls, a poem that Richard had written me and photos of my dad, brother and sister.

Advice from the Battlefield:

1. I recommend deep breathing and zero eye contact. I also try to find a focus point. Sometimes my focus point is my ex's ugly zip up shoes. It appears he has lost the ability to tie shoelaces since I left him.

2. I keep calm and focus on my children. I don't let myself get thrown into defending myself anymore. My lawyer told me to take a wee moment to collect my thoughts before answering and he also told me to stop talking after I answered the opposing lawyer's question. He told me that it is an old lawyer's ploy to stay silent after the question is answered. Otherwise, there is a good chance that you might get insecure and start

babbling. Short answers and then keep your mouth shut and endure the silence that might follow.

3. I have a Mother's Ring that my ex-narcissist gave me YEARS ago. I wear it on my middle finger <<wink>> of my right hand. I concentrate and focus on my 5 jewels and remember to focus on THEM and nothing else. Write down short, key points that you want/need to cover and check off as you go. Practice speaking out loud beforehand. Dress for court! Dress as you would for church or office. Hair up and/or out of face, light makeup, 'open your eyes' and let the Judge see that you have nothing to hide.

4. I have only been in court with him once, but I find I get activated in therapists' office, etc. I see it as an opportunity for me to practice a modified "gray rock;" to give no emotional information. I've done several things: practice a neutral phrase such as, "The shampoo is on the shelf" and make sure I pay attention to how my voice is. I then use that same voice when speaking about my ex, even when it produces anxiety in me: "He hasn't paid child support in ten months." to the 'tune' of "the shampoo sits on the shelf". I also pretend I am a very boring documentary narrator when saying things that are painful or that produce a reaction within me – even things he's done that are abusive or hurtful to the children. I've come to realize that the system is there to sift through the facts. We have already made our conclusions because we have lived it. But the system is not set up to deal with our conclusions, no matter how true and reasonable they are. So the more you can pull back and say your piece in such a way that leads people to the truth, the better you will be. It really does help to practice, too. In addition to the discernment about what to share when, the way you present your facts is helpful.

5. I always make sure I take someone with me that is a positive influence and that can calm me down. For me it is my dad. Although he is on my side, he is always pro child. He can see through the emotions and offers neutral outsider advice when needed. I also make sure I have a notebook with my goals and

what I want to accomplish. I also have an excellent attorney.

Mere Exposure Effect

In the very beginning of my battle, I spent a lot of time in the courtroom, and it wasn't solely based on the fact that I was embarking on a tumultuous high-conflict divorce. I planted myself in the courtroom to learn the ropes and to desensitize myself to the courtroom. I wanted to watch different cases and learn tips and strategies from respected attorneys.

The mere exposure effect is considered a psychological phenomenon in which a preference is developed by simply becoming familiar with an object or situation and the end result is comfort, reassurance and relief. While I did not have the goal of becoming so accustomed to court that I actually looked forward to going, I knew that familiarization would take the edge off and understanding the system would provide me with a sense of comfort.

Through this experience you can learn a lot of things about your particular Judge or Commissioner. In my case, I was told by a local paralegal that our particular Commissioner was somewhat biased against women who appeared to be damsels in distress. His viewpoint was, "You married him and now you want me to fix it?" While this was frustrating information, it was also helpful to know and understand the thoughts of the person deciding the future of my children and family. Obviously, I didn't agree with his stance but it gave me insight into the person in front of me.

Advice from the Battlefield:

1. I also spent time desensitizing myself to the courtroom. In addition, I spent a great deal of time reading WestLaw. I sat through open juvenile hearings, open divorce proceedings and custody cases. Some are closed or held in chambers when minors are involved which is why I spent time in the law library and studying WestLaw. I practiced with close friends and family to sharpen my skills pertaining to testifying, cross-examining and presenting evidence. I would also go to the domestic violence hearings. Whatever I could do to desensitize myself as much as I could, I did. I found all of these things to be very useful.

2. I didn't desensitize myself intentionally, but now, after 2.5 years of going, I don't get nervous or anxious at all and I can speak very clearly and calmly to the Judge. It would have been a good idea to spend some time sitting and watching 2.5 years ago for sure. Lawyers should recommend this.

3. I did a lot of research on my ex-wife's attorney in an attempt to prepare for what I was going up against in court. I joined a local support group for divorcees and spoke to others who had been up against this well-known attorney in court. I knew that this particular attorney would escalate things versus problem-solve and so I prepared myself for her approach. I responded with clear, factual answers to everything in person or via court documents. This experience was proof to me that sometimes it is more important to know the opposing attorney that it is to know your opponent.

4. Tina's genius Narc Decoder, which is featured on her blog, "One Mom's Battle," allowed me to understand the court documentation submitted by my ex-husband and to retain my composure regardless of how insane the accusations were. There are times (now) when I can read his court filings and laugh because I am so desensitized to the mad-man ramblings. This empowerment allows me to respond in a calm manner (after I've had a good laugh!).

5. In the beginning, I sat in the courtroom and honed in on the very high conflict cases. Once I had established a few cases which had undertones of my own case, I followed the cases and how the court reacted to certain things. I also found my new attorney through this process because I was able to watch them all in action. I found an attorney who was extremely qualified to go up against my ex-husband and his powerhouse legal team.

Muddy Water

I recently attended court with an OMB Warrior mom from my hometown. As I read her paperwork, I was amazed. It could have been written by Seth himself. Extra crispy bacon and fuzzy little bunnies: inside the mind of a narcissist. One technical term that I have developed to describe the narcissist's attempt to muddy the water in court is "extra crispy bacon and fuzzy bunnies." Confused? Me too. Why aren't the Judges confused? If I submitted paperwork accusing Seth of leaving my young daughters unattended in a swimming pool, he would muddy the waters with a response similar to this one:

"At 10:34 am on the day in question, the girls and I walked along a beautiful path similar to one that you would see in a fairytale. The girls were frolicking in the fresh green grass with fuzzy little bunnies (they had such cute pink noses!). After we enjoyed the birds, bunnies and three small ladybugs resting on a yellow daisy, we made our way to the swimming pool. At the pool, the girls and I played together and I never once took my gaze off of them. In addition, they were each wearing four life vests, two and a half arm floaties and each child had their very own swimming noodle which they never let go of. From there, we ate a very nutritious lunch consisting of veggie burgers with ketchup, mayonnaise and low fat bacon. The girls love bacon so much! Sarah likes hers very crispy and Piper prefers her on the softer side."

Pay no attention to the fact that the girls almost drowned because he fell asleep while hungover! Let him distract with fuzzy bunnies and details about how the girls like their bacon cooked! In addition to the normal rantings, ravings and fuzzy bunny stories, Seth was known to submit race results from triathlons he participated in to show that he was a legend in his own mind. At one point while trying to rationalize why he should not be subjected to guideline child support like common folk, he put together a profit & loss statement on our daughters. Sadly, it still took the courts over four years to see through his tactics.

Answers from the Battlefield:

1. In our pass-along book mine does the same thing…every visit with him is rainbows and cupcakes…everyone should ignore that terrible rash toddler returned with or the extreme thirst and hunger. My ex-narcissist will say which foods my child ate that she likes and dislikes, will lie about child napping or length of nap for purposes of showing that everything is perfect when she is with him. To me, it looks more idiotic to say that a toddler never gets frustrated or cranky when he/she is with you.

2. One of the narcissist's team members is the one who muddies the waters. To show the sheer absurdity of family court: In a session with GAL, before court (not knowing yet she was biased with ex,) I light-heartedly repeated the expression, "If mama ain't happy, ain't nobody happy." When we get to court, GAL testifies to the Judge, "Your Honor, Maryanne has said, if she wasn't happy, no one was going to be happy." I swear this happened. Lesson to be learned, you really have to be very conscious of every word you speak. As well as to not naively place your trust.

3. Most people who know me think I am a kind-hearted, giving person. In court one day I sat behind my narcissistic ex-son-in-law who was trying to pin onto me the nasty behaviors (emotional abuse and brainwashing) that he and his mother perpetrated on the little ones during their summer parenting time. Supposedly, I achieved this deviousness while driving a car with the CPS worker beside me in the front seat, on the way to hospital for physical exams for children, who were in the back seat with their mother (my daughter). In that 30-minute car trip I supposedly accomplished what it took the narcissist and his minions six weeks to complete. He claimed this in an effort to discredit my daughter. When the narcissist realized the Judge, GAL, and CPS were not buying that explanation, he became beet red, talking loudly and described me as "a dangerous subversive!" I remember trying not to smile, shaking my head while making eye contact with the Judge who, two minutes later, informed the narcissist that should my daughter be unable to care for the children, I was their legal guardian.

4. My favorite moment was during his cross examination of myself on the stand. He brought up how he had been accused by the ministry of safety issues and neglect. He made a big show, implying the accusations were over-exaggerated and claimed I had much worse disregard for the children's safety – he had proof in the form of a photo taken from my Facebook. He passed it around to the Judge, my lawyer, and finally to myself on the stand. I had no idea what it was. I broke a sweat –

had I really done something terrible? I didn't think I had... One look at the photo and I nearly laughed out loud. He began to describe it for the court. "Clearly you can see Juliette jumping with another adult on a trampoline, our children sitting on the sides watching, their backs to the edge. These children could have fallen to the ground, bounced off and been injured" Then it was my turn to reply. "Your Honor," I said, "this trampoline is flush with the ground. It's actually at a campground for disabled children. It is impossible for them to fall off." The narcissist actually had a moment of speechlessness. It was pure awesome.

5. My ex-husband called the police thinking I was home alone and explained to the officer that I had sent him a text message claiming that I was going to kill myself. When the officers arrived, I was preparing to take my sick daughter to a doctor's appointment! The police came in and didn't even need to check house because I was dressed and my daughter stated that we were on our way to an appointment. The house was spotless and in order. Hardly a woman on the verge of taking her life. The police actually laughed at the situation. I asked if it is illegal what he did, falsely stating what he did and wasting police time, all to think he was going to get a report on me to try once again to get custody so he doesn't have to pay child support. The police were just happy I was okay. He also called my employer on the same day and told her (my boss) the same story. She told him she just talked to me and that I was taking his daughter to the doctor and he answered her "My daughter is home sick?" Unreal.

Discovery Process

During this period of time both parties are busy gathering information about the other side. If there is ever a time when you can legally be stalked, this would be it. While you should *never* use social media to vent about your divorce or custody battle, it is especially important to stop if you are dealing with a high conflict personality. Anything and everything you write, post or tweet can and will be used against you. Feel free to talk about the weather or post inspirational quotes but do not discuss your divorce or anything else that can be twisted or taken out of context.

You will need to become a private investigator when it comes to collecting information. During our divorce proceedings, I was able to find incriminating Facebook postings such as Seth snowboarding in Utah while claiming poverty. I collected information about his drinking from local bar-goers without even trying very hard. A friend's babysitter happened to be showing her photos from Halloween and in one photo, there was a costume-clad Darth Vader passed out cold on the floor of a Mexican food restaurant. Apparently, Seth had a few too many margaritas that night. I even discovered his dating profile on a Fitness Singles site which bragged about his income, the homes that he owned and the fact that he had never been married nor did he have children. Yes, that one went over well in the midst of a child custody evaluation.

One of the huge victories in protecting my daughters came in 2011 when Seth was lying to the court about the whereabouts of the girls during his visitation. Unbeknownst to Seth, minor's counsel, or the Commissioner, I had equipped the girls with a cell phone which had GPS tracking. I let him paint his fuzzy bunny story about where they were and then I provided GPS tracking records to show where they really went. To catch him lying to the Commissioner was a huge blow to his case and, essentially, ended his overnight visits permanently.

There were multiple occasions when I hired private investigators to follow Seth on the nights before his visits. He was often so hungover during his parenting time that he napped for extended periods of time and left the children unattended. It was my word against his and anything that the children said was hearsay. A private detective was the one person who could follow Seth and document exactly how much alcohol he was drinking prior to his big debut as a father for a mere six hours, four days per month. I found it quite sad and pathetic that he couldn't even pull himself together for the brief periods of time that he saw our daughters.

Advice from the Battlefield:

1. I searched social media. I documented when he cancelled his parenting time (he wasn't paying any child support) but posted about the bars, concerts, and festivals he attended. I saw the

pictures of him and the kids out together without his parents'
(court ordered) supervision. Meaning it was very likely he had
also violated the court order about transporting the children (he
was banned). I saw the business he started but did not report in
court. I had the text messages he sent about making money in
that business. I had pictures of him working at another job
which he also had denied in court even though a family member
acknowledged it to the GAL. I saw where he claimed to have a
college degree that I knew was false. The GAL contacted the
college who verified he had never taken a class there. It all
converged to paint a picture of a liar who refused to obey the
court's directives.

2. Let's face it: a private detective is expensive but at times it is a
    necessity. I hired mine to follow me. Yes, you read that right.
    My ex was stalking me and his friends were lying in wait for
    me and following me, etc. My PI became my "security
    detail" who could document the BS. I supplement his stuff with
    recording devices purchased off eBay, mini spy cams, apps, etc.
    The evidence will hopefully prove to be invaluable. Either way,
    it helps show my ex-husband for the fruit loop he is. I also hired
    the PI because my ex-husband and his new wife are both police
    officers. I chose my PI because I felt comfortable with him, but
    also because he was a retired police officer. I hired experienced
    cop(s) versus rookies that are liars. I hope to have good news to
    report at my next court date as this evidence is the heart of my
    case.

3. In regards to the state of intoxication.... most Judges will order
    a 24 hour prior-to and during order restricting the use of
    intoxicants unless prescribed by physician, pending proof. In
    most cases proving the emotional instability to properly parent
    under the influence (this includes hungover) rests on the
    protecting parent to provide. Depending on the level of
    dependency, the psychological damage on the children could
    limit the other parent's access significantly. Any and all
    documentation proving fraudulent acts of his paint a pretty
    picture of his lack of responsibility and deceitfulness, which

discredits anything he brings to the table. It also brings to question morals and parenting practices. Children are a product of their environment, and subjecting them to the risk of emotional abuse (which is what addicts are very versed at) is not in their best interest. This evidence is all in your favor.

4. Most incriminating, publicly posted items were found on the sites of his girlfriends (aka flying monkeys). Once they opened the channel to stalk me, I was able to peruse their FB posts. There were the pictures of tropical vacations and out of state parties attended with his various liaisons before I knew my marriage was in trouble. After the divorce proceedings started, I Googled myself and my property records, had the IRS run a check on me, and had my bank run a credit report on me. A ton of useful, publicly available information came to light. I highly recommend it.

5. One thing that helped me was his "favorite past time" smoking, as he put it, a "harmless plant." I just offered a drug test each time he wanted visitation and he would back off. I documented all his failed visits also as failed drug test compliance. He was court ordered to drug test but he never did anything about that, either (too much work for him). Showing all the missed visits was enough to get full custody, but not taking even one drug test offered helped me to gain supervised visits.

Witness Declarations

I have discovered that there are two types of people when it comes to collecting written declarations from witnesses during custody battles. There are people who are willing to talk and shouldn't and there are people who should talk but refuse to do so. Both are equally frustrating for a variety of reasons.

I struggled to understand how a person who knows nothing about a situation can be so eager to get involved. Seth went on a hunt for anyone who would jot down nice things about him including, but not limited to, a single mother whom he was trying to impress and a doctor whom he met while swimming at the local athletic club. Thankfully, these declarations are not highly regarded by the courts as most people are able to collect statements like this.

The statements which are considered by the courts are statements that show actual examples of good parenting or defects in character. These are two actual examples of character statements submitted by Seth's former friend who, to this day, I've never met and another from his ex-girlfriend:

> *"While at a concert with my friends on July 16 2011, Seth became heavily intoxicated and began displaying irate and verbally abusive behavior towards myself and my friends. He was accusing us of interfering with his desire to date my friend, Amanda while completely disregarding Amanda's explicit refusal to engage in any form of relationship with him. After the event ended, Seth demanded that we listen to his apology in regards to his disturbing behavior and then insisted on driving us to a bar. Due to his heavy alcohol consumption and insistence on driving, we were concerned and finally persuaded him to allow a sober person to drive his car. Upon arrival at the bar, I was increasingly uncomfortable with his drunkenness and left the establishment."* –Former Friend

> *"Shortly after New Year's Eve, our relationship ended. When I told Seth that I no longer wanted to see him, he became completely irrational. He would not accept the fact that I was breaking up with him and tried to physically fight one of my male friends. He then began calling my employer and disparaging me in an attempt to make me lose my job. I became increasingly concerned about Seth's behavior and my personal safety. I began receiving multiple hateful voice messages, text messages and long letters. I was so concerned and fearful of Seth by this point that I was forced to change the locks on the doors to my home. While dating Seth, I found him to be delusional and emotionally irrational by jumping from fake happiness to extreme anger."* -Former Girlfriend

While one or two statements like this is not enough, a variety of examples helps to substantiate claims of alcohol abuse and unstable mental health. On the reverse side, gathering statements from church leaders, school teachers, childcare providers or other reputable people are highly recommended. The burden of proving your parenting is on you as the court will not have time to look into this nor will they take your word for it. As a reminder, facts always outweigh character witnesses.

Advice from the Battlefield:

1. I only had close family and my psychiatrist provide witness statements. I had moral support from one of my friends but I never asked her to provide any witness statements. She was there with me through the worst of the court sessions. He, on the other hand, had numerous character witness statements (most of which were denied any weight as these people weren't ever directly related to me – not reliable). Then he went to an ex friend as well as his misogynistic army buddy and mistress to provide witness statements which were libelous, character-assassinating, emotionally-fueled and largely based on hearsay rather than actual fact. Because of this, the credibility of his witnesses was less than favorable. I made sure to stick to hard facts and leave the emotion out of it. It paid off in the end.

2. I had two witnesses that could have helped me but due to an emergency hearing my ex-husband placed on the court calendar, they were unable to come. The most frustrating thing, however, was those who knew about the abuse and refused to step forward. Each came up with a reason but I believe they just didn't want to get involved and I believe one or two were actually scared of the narcissist. I cannot say I blame them as I was afraid of him too. Due to this, however, I was determined to be a good witness to anyone who needed it.

3. I've learned that anyone you have sitting in the courtroom as personal support during any one of the hearings will be ruled as biased and not allowed to be a witness for your final hearing.

4. Getting my daughters established in therapy from the very beginning was essential. Therapists are mandated reporters and can become a "safe person" to children in the midst of divorce chaos. A qualified play therapist can even take on children under the age of two years old. I spoke to teachers, principals, pediatricians and therapists in the very beginning and let them know that their job was to advocate for my children – not take

sides with either parent. My goal from the beginning was for the courts to truly decide what was in the best interest of my children and, thankfully, they had a team of people in place who became their voice when they needed it most. Another thing that I learned, which may vary from state to state, is that a pediatrician has the legal authority to approve therapy sessions even if one parent is refusing to authorize sessions. It is that way in my state, which allowed me to bypass my ex-husband who didn't want our children in therapy. In my opinion, this alone was a red flag to the court – what parent wouldn't want their child to receive therapy if it is obviously needed? My children's therapist wrote the most compelling declaration that my attorney had seen in 20 years.

5. I personally collected as much evidence (by email and text) as possible from two witnesses who were willing to provide me with information yet refused to put it in writing for the courts. After a venting session to my limited scope attorney, she looked at me and said, "We will subpoena them!" In my frustration, I never even thought of this as an option! I found that one witness was relieved because being subpoenaed showed that she was not giving up the information voluntarily. The second witness said (on the stand) that she had been hesitant to come forward because she had been threatened by my husband and lived in fear of him. That statement also helped to paint the picture of who my ex-husband was.

Custody Evaluations

During the course of my battle, we had a total of two full custody evaluations. The initial evaluation took place in 2010 which was before I understood NPD or the severity of what I was dealing with. I went into the evaluation unprepared and naïve, and was assigned a case worker who was close to retiring and completely inept when it came to understanding the situation in front of her. I was finally awarded a second custody evaluation. That was the result of thirteen court dates in 2012 and a Commissioner who was tired of hearing from us and overwhelmed with the he-said, she-said accusations.

Our second custody evaluation began in January of 2013, right around the time my first book, "Divorcing a Narcissist: One Mom's Battle" was hitting the book shelves. This particular evaluation was like night and day compared to the first one. By this point in time, I knew exactly who and what I was dealing with. In addition, there had been clear patterns established which made it much easier for the evaluator to have a clear picture of the past four years of our custody battle. The evaluator himself also made a world of difference. Not only was he competent and educated on high-conflict personalities, to me, he was living proof that there was hope for the Family Court System.

I felt very confident going into the evaluation because the Commissioner had given us each an opportunity to list the concerns that we wanted investigated. Seth's concerns focused on my book, my blog and his conviction that the children were being alienated by the publicity surrounding our case. In other words, his main concerns rested in the fact that I was publically outing him. That is the worst thing that you can do to a narcissist.

I was speechless and felt incredibly thankful while reading the final list of items that the Commissioner ordered to be investigated:

- Whether father's behavior is causing the children to experience fear or anxiety.

- Whether mother's behavior is causing the children to experience fear or anxiety.

- Whether mother's blog/website is causing difficulties for the children or is likely to cause the children to experience difficulty or dysfunction.

- Whether father's conduct, recently or historically, during visitation has posed a risk of harm to the children.

- Whether the children have been physically or emotionally abused while in their father's care.

- Whether the children have been physically or emotionally abused while in their mother's care.

- Obtain documentation of father's use or abuse of alcohol and

investigate circumstances surrounding car accident in
September of 2011.

- Interview witnesses as to father's anger issues, hostility and
rationality in daily living, and his use or abuse of alcohol or
drugs.

- Attempt to obtain "harassing" emails sent from father to ex-
girlfriends.

- Investigate whether records from couple's former marriage
counselor documents injury related to oldest child.

- Interview former nannies who lived with the family to obtain
information related to alcohol abuse and neglect.

- Interview father's former landlord as to father's stability,
mental state and whether, and to what extent, father "staged
their mutual home" for the 2010 parenting evaluation.

- Investigate father's 2011 DUI and determine if this event
happened on his visitation weekend.

- Investigate whether children have free access to their cell phone
while in their father's care and if they've always had free
access.

- Investigate what the reasons are, if any, that the children should
not be allowed to be in the home of the father's older brother.

- What orders would be in the best interest of the children with
respect to custody and visitation?

The Commissioner had finally reviewed our entire file. He must have sat
down with all five volumes of our court file and combed through all of my
accusations dating back to 2009. I was in complete shock as I read the order.
This was it. This was the break that we needed. Not only did we have a
thorough set of items to be investigated, but we had an investigator who was
highly regarded by the court due to his expertise and integrity. This
investigator was hand selected by the Commissioner because he was the one
person who could get to the bottom of these issues.

The concerns about One Mom's Battle were quickly dismissed by the evaluator when it was revealed that I had gone above and beyond to protect the children from my writings. The girls knew that I had written a book but didn't even know the title. I was able to show how proactive I had been in keeping them from my advocacy, my blog and the book. In fact, I had gone so far as to install K-9 parental controls on our home computers which blocked my writings and books from even showing up.

During the investigation, which spanned over six months, I experienced a life-changing gift that came right in the midst of our custody evaluation. It all began with an early morning email in March of 2013 from a physician in California who had stayed up overnight reading my first book. As it turns out, my book helped her to make sense of her courtship, marriage and divorce and because of that, she felt pulled to help me in my own battle. This "angel" came into my life and believed in me enough to not only locate an exceptional attorney but to also pay my legal fees for the upcoming trial which had my stomach in knots. While I had represented myself for over four years, I felt like everything was riding on this evaluation and the pending trial which was accompanied by a level of anxiety that I had never experienced before.

This particular lawyer brought forth experience as a prosecuting attorney in addition to her role as a Family Court litigator, which was a combination made in courtroom heaven. There are two things that had become solid over the course of my custody battle: my backbone and my faith. Where I once lacked boundaries and the ability to stand up for myself, I grew stronger each year and surprised myself with the inner strength that I grew to possess. Going into this battle, I could have been considered an atheist by definition. Thankfully, the beginning of my battle brought forth an unexpected chain of events that landed me smack dab in the pews of a local church. With each passing month, my faith grew and I knew beyond a shadow of a doubt that God had placed me on this path to help others. I credit God for the angel in my life, the custody evaluator, and the fact that I finally had an attorney when I needed one the most.

Prior to my first meeting with the Custody Evaluator, I worked hard to prepare a list to keep myself on track. I compiled my evidence in an easy-to-read, bullet-point format based on the court order of items to be investigated. I arrived to the appointment 20 minutes early and did three things before I left my car: I said a prayer for the truth to prevail, I took deep breaths and I made sure that I was emotionally centered. I walked into that first meeting repeating the quote, "Speak the truth, even if your voice shakes."

After the first meeting, which lasted over two hours, I had an additional meeting, and throughout the investigation my daughters were interviewed multiple times. There was a home visit at my house and another home visit at the location that Seth had staged within weeks of receiving the evaluation order. Seth didn't even live in the county, yet his family came together to assist him in creating a fake residence where he set up wooden birdhouses for the girls to paint while the investigator visited his "home." The thought of Seth doing crafts with the girls was laughable at best. Things like this left me feeling desperate yet hopeful that the evaluator would see through Seth's façade.

During every encounter with Seth, he would say things like, "I am so happy that they are finally getting to the bottom of this once and for all. They are going to see right through you and prove that you are alienating and damaging the girls." I had to reassure myself that he normally acts the most confident and cocky when he is scared. The old me would have left feeling shaken and worried but the new me, thoroughly educated on NPD, walked away feeling even more hopeful. I, too, was grateful that they were finally getting to the bottom of things, but my confidence was based on my truth and my faith. I knew that Seth lacked both of those things.

During the months before our final trial date, I began to pray like I had never prayed before. I prayed in the car, in the shower, in bed and even got down on my knees. I visualized the outcome that I wanted and then I prayed more. I knew in my heart that the only thing that would keep my daughters safe was professionally supervised visits. I had been told by everyone that it was a long shot but I was not going to accept that as a long shot. In my mind, supervised visits were the only acceptable answer in this equation.

Just weeks before the trial date, I was anxiously awaiting the results of the evaluation when something happened that would change the outcome of our case in a way that I never anticipated. As the girls climbed into my car after a visit with their father, my oldest daughter said something that I will never forget: "Mom, Dad was drinking alcohol today. He was drinking beer at lunch. He lied and said it was soda but I heard the waitress say, 'Here is your beer'." To make matters worse, I discovered that he had actually taken the girls into a bar for lunch and his parents were also present and drinking. After drinking beer, he put the girls in the car and drove them to our exchange location.

I was in disbelief over what I was hearing. Alcohol had played such a large role in our marriage and throughout our custody battle. The court order was incredibly clear: Seth was not allowed to drink alcohol for the six hours preceding the visits and there was to be absolutely no alcohol around the girls during his visits. The fact that he took them into a bar and drank alcohol while our custody evaluation was underway blew my mind and showed me that he was once again above court orders. I had made comments along the way that nothing Seth did could shock me anymore but I was wrong. I couldn't believe that he had just given me the final piece that I needed to protect my daughters.

I sprung into action because I knew the clock was ticking. I immediately emailed the custody evaluator and scheduled an appointment for him to interview my daughters. I secured the GPS record of my daughter's phone, which substantiated her claims that they were in a bar. I then called the private investigator who had been following Seth on and off for weeks and hired him to go to the bar and talk to the manager about obtaining surveillance video of Seth drinking, along with the receipt for Seth's purchases.

If there was one thing I've learned in this battle it is to have concrete, black and white evidence. Grey matter is preferred by the narcissist because it gives them wiggle room to lie and manipulate, but it doesn't fly in court. I was *not* going to risk the court saying that my daughters' account of the incident was hearsay. I wanted the Commissioner to watch Seth drinking beer in a bar with my daughters. I wanted the Commissioner to see Seth's parents drinking in the bar – the same parents who promised that they would ensure that Seth obeyed court orders at all times. I wanted the Commissioner to watch them all blatantly defying court orders. I wanted the Commissioner to see Seth's narcissism firsthand.

The private investigator, another angel in my life, was able to make contact with the GM of the Irish Pub where Seth had been drinking. The GM knew Seth well and immediately expressed his dislike for him. John, the private investigator, was able to view the surveillance video and verify that Seth was shown drinking. However, we needed to secure approval from the owner of the pub before we could take the video with us. Once again, I sprung into action and called everyone that I knew to try and connect with the restaurant owner. In the meantime, my new attorney was preparing a subpoena to attempt to obtain the video in time for court which was now just two days away.

The fact that my entire head of hair didn't go gray this particular week still amazes me. I was operating in fight or flight mode and would have probably benefited from some type of anti-anxiety medication. While I was officially in overdrive, I was still waiting to hear if the custody evaluation would even be done in time for court. On Tuesday, July 9th, just 24 hours before court, my attorney called and my heart stopped. I immediately pulled my car over to the side of the road and took the call that would change everything. I listened intently as she read me the most important pieces of the report. I was in shock. The investigator got it. He saw through Seth. There were 43 pages in the report which completely validated every sleepless night, every claim of abuse that was inflicted on my daughters and every concern that I had ever expressed.

I hung up the phone and began to sob. I called every one of my friends and family members until my phone battery was completely drained. I would have climbed up on the nearest rooftop and started shouting had I been able to find a ladder. The investigator was strongly recommending professionally supervised visits along with a myriad of other stipulations which I knew that Seth would never agree to. I also knew that the Commissioner finally had everything that he needed to protect my children. The report could not have been any better had I personally written all 43 pages.

I arrived in court on the morning of July 10, 2013 and immediately saw Seth, his attorney and his parents, Leonard and Cleo. We had fully prepared ourselves for Seth's attorney to ask for a continuance because he had eluded to needing one based on the fact that he hadn't had ample time to review the custody evaluation. My attorney was prepared to ask for supervised visits pending the final review hearing. In my heart of hearts, I was devastated because I couldn't imagine another wait.

There was another person pacing in the courtroom and based on his demeanor, I could tell that he was not there willingly. The gentleman was the GM of the Irish Pub and in his hand was the surveillance video which my attorney had successfully subpoenaed. The attorneys all agreed to meet privately in chambers. From that moment on, the next hour felt like a complete whirlwind.

After about 30 minutes, the attorneys and the Commissioner re-entered the courtroom. I quickly noticed that Seth and his father were not present. My attorney told me that Seth's attorney was going to agree to ALL of the Evaluator's recommendations. While they had agreed to supervised visits, Seth's attorney was requesting that Cleo, Seth's mother, be allowed to supervised. No. No. No. I quickly told my attorney that I was adamantly opposed to this. Seth's mom had been in the bar and was drinking with him — she knew they were in violation of the court order and she participated in violating the order. I couldn't believe they had the gall to even ask this of the court.

When the Commissioner spoke, he stated that Seth's mother and father have been a part of this case from the beginning and they were fully aware of the court orders. He stated that he would absolutely NOT approve Seth's mother to monitor the visits. He then said words that I will never forget: "The following orders are FINAL custody orders. Professionally supervised visits – 1st, 3rd and 5th weekends per month"

> *"Evidence has been presented in support of a request that the contact of 'Seth' be supervised based upon allegations of physical abuse, alcohol abuse, use of threats and tendency to be dishonest. The court intends for this to be a final custody order."*

It took everything in me not to scream. It was over. My battle was over!!!!!! My daughters were safe!

As we left the courtroom, I was advised that Seth had become the Tasmanian Devil on the steps of the courtroom. Apparently, he was huffing, puffing and yelling that he was going to start videotaping my every move. That would prove to be a fairly uneventful documentary entitled, "A day in the life of a working mom," but I wish him well with that endeavor.

To further show how disturbing the mind of a narcissist is, I was in shock when I heard Seth's excuse for drinking in a bar with the girls. *It was all a test.* He claimed that he was setting us up. He said he was testing the girls to see if they would report the information back to me. Someday I may write a book called, "Yes, the Narcissist really said that." Ironically, his mother had already admitted to our evaluator that they were drinking because had she not, his answer would have been different. His answer would have probably been complete and utter denial.

After the final judgment, I spent several days in utter shock. It was the exact verdict that I had hoped and prayed for but I wasn't prepared. I expected court to be delayed for another month. Everything happened so fast and I wasn't even a part of it. The attorneys handled everything and I felt like I was caught in a tornado of commotion. Spinning and so fast – it was over. My girls were safe.

I left the courtroom and felt dazed. I didn't cry. I was elated, but I didn't cry. I had always expected that a moment like this would bring a flood of tears so vast that a dam would need to be constructed in the town square. Days later, I was still dazed and fuzzy. The only way I could explain it to people was that there was a "block" – I felt that my emotions were blocked and it wasn't sinking in. I couldn't grasp the concept that my children were finally safe and that we would have peace. I didn't even know what peace would feel like. Let me be the first to tell you, peace is an amazing thing and I wish this feeling for everyone who has battled this storm.

I often discourage people in my support group from making blanket statements about the Family Court System, attorneys or others who have a hand in deciding the fate of a child. All Judges are not bad and all Custody Evaluators are not bad. I agree that the vast majority is corrupt, uneducated or generally disconnected but they aren't all bad. I thank God for aligning me with a Custody Evaluator who wasn't bought by the NPD charm and who truly worked to ensure that the best interest of the child was his motivating factor.

Overall, you need to think forensically when preparing for a Custody Evaluation. Being well-organized is imperative and mandatory. Make sure that your files and documents are labeled properly and organized in an easy-to-find method. I personally had things broken down by year and prioritized by significance, which allowed me to show a pattern over a period of time. I then put together a master timeline of events and occurrences which guided the evaluator through our journey. I highlighted things that I wanted him to focus on and I tried very hard not to overwhelm him, which is a very fine line.

Individuals with Narcissistic Personality Disorder are prone to long, rambling explanations in which they talk in circles and avoid answering direct questions. Taking the opposite stance by submitting verifiable, factual information and answering truthfully will speak volumes to the evaluator without actually writing volumes. Honesty is not only the best policy when it comes to speaking to the evaluator, it is the *only* policy. One false statement, no matter how small it may seem, can ensure that you lose all credibility in short order.

Obviously this is my personal opinion, but if your ex has not been diagnosed with a personality disorder, do NOT try to self-diagnose him. This is not your field of expertise nor are you his psychologist. Doing so can actually come back to haunt you in a big way. If you suspect that your ex has a personality disorder or even very high narcissistic traits than what you *can* do is provide examples of each behavior as they relate to your custody case. However, avoid openly self-diagnosing at all costs.

The Diagnostic and Statistical Manual of Mental Disorders fourth edition, DSM IV-TR, a widely-used manual for diagnosing mental disorders, defines narcissistic personality disorder (in Axis II Cluster B) as:

> A pervasive pattern of grandiosity (in fantasy or behavior), need for admiration, and lack of empathy, beginning by early adulthood and present in a variety of contexts, as indicated by five (or more) of the following:
>
> - Has a grandiose sense of self-importance (e.g., exaggerates achievements and talents, expects to be recognized as superior without commensurate achievements).
>
> - Is preoccupied with fantasies of unlimited success, power, brilliance, beauty, or ideal love.
>
> - Believes that he or she is "special" and unique and can only be understood by, or should associate with, other special or high-status people (or institutions).

- Requires excessive admiration.

- Has a sense of entitlement, i.e., unreasonable expectations of especially favorable treatment or automatic compliance with his or her expectations.

- Is inter-personally exploitative, i.e., takes advantage of others to achieve his or her own ends.

- Lacks empathy: is unwilling to recognize or identify with the feelings and needs of others.

- Is often envious of others or believes others are envious of him or her.

- Shows arrogant, haughty behavior or attitudes.

It is further a requirement of DSM-IV that a diagnosis of any specific personality disorder also satisfies a set of general personality disorder criteria. Please refer to the DSM-IV for the criteria and remember that a diagnosis is only credible and admissible from a licensed provider.

My custody evaluation was extremely thorough and the evaluator was open and willing to speak to witnesses who could testify to Seth's behavior, anger issues and alcohol abuse. I obtained a detailed list of individuals who could attest to my character, mothering and community involvement. The individuals on my list were preschool teachers, school principals, friends, local business owners, employers and others who knew me well. In addition to the character reference list that Seth submitted, I provided the Evaluator with my own list of character references for him such as ex-girlfriends, ex-roommates and mutual friends who had had run-ins with him over the years. Painting a clear picture of the Narcissist is essential.

As Jamie, our One Mom's Battle Administrator likes to say, *"Know your desired outcome going into it... thread it with consistency... think forensically."*

Advice from the Battlefield:

1. Be completely honest about your own mistakes. Your ex will have made notes about everything you've done and will try to use it against you. If the evaluator hears your honesty, they'll be

more likely to believe what you say about your ex. None of us is a perfect parent, and they know it. Also, don't be afraid to sound like you're boasting by talking about your positive qualities as a parent. You have the right to tell people why you're a good mom. I found being honest really helped me in the end. The ex made things up about me, but never took responsibility for any mistakes he made. Document EVERYTHING, but stick to facts. Don't add commentary. Remain confident in your parenting skills.

2. First ask around to make sure you get a highly respected evaluator. Be brutally honest and transparent. Appear organized and well put together. Turn papers in on time. Follow any suggestions they give to the letter. Take responsibility for your part of things, your mistakes. It is hard at first, but if you are lucky, as I was, your narcissist will only be able to lie and pretend he is someone else for a little while. I would get so upset by the lies he was telling and the things he would say, but a wise friend kept telling me not to react or get defensive. To tell him I was sorry he felt that way, and give him the rope to hang himself. And guess what, he did. Our evaluation took 6 months and in the end, the evaluator's report showed a pattern of verbal and emotional abuse and control, he markered for narcissism on the psych exam and eluded to PAS. Her recommendation was for me to be given back my kids, joint custody. Be prepared for him to contest the 730 evaluation report if it is not in his favor. Ultimately you will end up having a trial, but I have heard it is rare that the Judge throws the report out. He/she usually accepts part, if not all, of report as evidence and adopts the evaluator's recommendations.

3. The first question is whether this is a private agency or a county agency? I've had both and both had very different methods. The private agency was $40,000.00 and charged to investigate per accusation. Given that there was nearly 138 false accusations at $200 per hour, you can see how quickly this can add up. Then, I had a county agency because I couldn't afford the private custody evaluations. They charged $2,000.00, read

nearly every paper and quickly dismissed the outrageous
slander. The county didn't get PAID to increase the acrimony.
They did their job professionally and even though I disagreed
with 10% of the report, it helped to bring down the conflict
level.

4. My advice.... it depends on the circumstances. Sadly, most
   often protective parents are drained of their resources by the
   diligent bilking done by the "justice system," leaving them with
   limited financial options. That being said, often times the
   evaluator is assigned by the court. As soon as you can find out
   the name of the evaluator, begin researching cases he or she has
   been involved with. There are groups everywhere that keep
   working lists of custody evaluators. Far too often these
   professionals are simply tools of the court that will aid the side
   the Judge is leaning towards. In a case in upstate New York
   where abuse was a key topic for the protective parent, the
   evaluator was on record as having stated that "abuse allegations
   were false in the majority of cases." She showed the bias of the
   court long before the actual ruling. What is worse is that in the
   above case (New York), the evaluator was flown in from
   Florida specifically for the case rather than using one locally,
   which made it virtually impossible to be able to dispute the
   findings. My advice is to do the research, find out who it is and
   what type of person they are. Once you've got a solid
   understanding of what you are facing you can better prepare for
   the treachery of a family court evaluator.

5. I have learned a great deal during my own custody evaluation:

   a. Listen carefully to the questions, take a minute to
      form your response before speaking, answer
      honestly and don't embellish. If you can't
      remember then say so and ask to look back in your
      journal.

   b. Don't badmouth/diagnose or say anything
      slanderous about the ex. Provide your PROOF of
      misdeeds/law enforcement through your journals.

c. Don't offer information (I tend to over-talk when I get nervous) and there were downtimes in the interviews that I would have normally tried to fill with small talk which would have taken time away from the reason we were there. It would not have been beneficial.

d. If asked to provide letters of recommendations, make sure the people you choose know that they need to write about YOU and not to slander the ex. Same with family interviews.

e. Be human. Everyone makes mistakes in life and parenting, so don't beat yourself up if something is brought to light. Turn it, spin it and let the counselor know what you have changed/done/learned from the bad. I had a positive (though nerve-wracking) experience with the process: she was the one who diagnosed my ex with NPD. She went above and beyond to protect my teens and myself from his backlash when the report came out. My ex came in there seething with contempt for me, my family, and the process. He puffed out his chest and tried to record their conversation (without her knowledge)...it cost him...though if you ask him he will tell you he won a great victory. He lost time with his kids but pays less to support them and to him that is a win. (We both had attorneys)

Child Welfare Services

It is my hope and dream that all 50 states will follow in Arizona's footsteps as they demand a full overhaul on Child Welfare Services (CWS), also referred to as the Department of Children and Family Services (DCSF) or Child Protective Services (CPS) in some states. In my role as an advocate, I hear the worst of the worst but I also hear positive stories about Judges who are acting in the best interest of the child or Minor's Counsel who seems to really understand personality disorders. I hear about Custody Evaluators who go the extra mile or attorneys who are truly making a difference. There is one segment of the Family Court System that doesn't seem to receive glowing reviews: Child Welfare Services.

This is an agency that has no accountability and their power is terrifying. Speak out or confront them and risk losing custody of your children, yet when they need to act, they don't. I am generally against blanket statements and while I do believe that there are CWS Social Workers and employees who are heart-driven and in it for the right reasons, I believe that the entire system needs an overhaul. My personal experience with this agency in San Luis Obispo County has left me feeling frustrated, desperate and reeling. Despite three reports (two called in from mandated reporters), they closed the cases and labeled them "unfounded." How can a case be labeled unfounded when the perpetrator actually admits to the accusations?

For over a year, I have stayed in touch with a mother who has been involved with Monroe County CPS in New York. There have been weekends where I am personally on edge and heartbroken while awaiting updates that her son is okay after visiting with his father. Despite 14 or more reports to CPS, including reports filed by mandated reporters, this little boy is placed in the care of an incredibly abusive and mentally ill father. I have seen photos of his burned and bruised body yet no one will help him. This case literally makes me ill. This is an excerpt of his story:

> It is a typical Monday morning as I get my son ready for school, having his clothes all laid out the evening before. I get him out of bed to get him dressed as I do every morning. My little blonde haired son, big blue eyes, trying to fight back the tears, shakes his head. "No mommy, I don't want to wear that shirt today to school."
>
> "It is your favorite shirt, Monster Jam."
>
> "No mommy."
>
> He goes over to his dresser to pull out a long sleeve shirt and hands it to me as his eyes fill up with tears. I have seen that look so many Monday mornings. The routine has become too familiar.
>
> As I slowly take his shirt off, our eyes fixed on each other, both fighting back the tears that are welling up in our eyes, trying to

hide the bruises. Bruises that he got on his weekend visit with someone that is supposed to love him. Without him saying one word to me, I know where those bruises came from. They are all over his little body, some big, some small. As I finish getting him dressed, he gives me a big hug and whispers in my ear, "Thank you Mommy. Now no one will see my boo boos."

I give him a big hug and say "I love you, Buddy."

This is what I think of when I read about the Kansas "spanking bill" 2699. This is what I think about when I read anything that normalizes or endorses corporal punishment. As long is corporal punishment against children is used, it will be over-used. The state officials who I've turned to in order to protect my son have told me again and again "corporal punishment is legal in New York." What is considered "excessive" is a matter of opinion. It's the State's opinion.

It's my son. And he's hurt.

Advice from the Battlefield:

1. CPS was worse than any narcissistic psychopath I ever dealt with because they actually DO have power, and they abuse it endlessly. I have a LOT to say about them and none of it is good. From what I saw, money was a big factor. It was THE deciding factor. I never saw a person of wealth sitting in those court rooms trying to get their children back. I saw the poor and vulnerable. That tells me a lot right there. My ex-husband physically abused my child and I went to the hospital for help. Not the police, not social services. The hospital. When my ex-husband was called for questioning, the tables were turned on me and I was called the abuser. It goes deep, and my child and I were both severely traumatized by them. They lied, they created crisis, they beat and battered me down so bad I've never been able to pick myself back up. Because of them, I lost my home, my cars, my child, my family. I had three jobs I was fired from because I couldn't keep up with full-time work to meet all their demands. They destroyed my son, our relationship and my life.

I was about to escape my abuse, and they threw me back into the wolf pit, and it was worse than it ever was before. It has been 6 years now since they destroyed us, and I haven't seen my son for 3 of those years. I WAS a good mom and they turned me into a monster. It has been an absolute, horrific nightmare dealing with them. My son and I would be abuse-free right now if it wasn't for social services. Everything I said was ignored. Every cry for help was met with pure contempt. I was bullied, degraded, dehumanized, and threatened. My rights were violated. They broke laws to keep us a part, re-wrote history, forced me to sign things with use of threats. They very people who were supposed to protect us from abuse re-created it all a million times worse. They clung to every word my ex-husband said and used it as absolute truth.
The truth is, Social Services has NO clue about what it means to actually be abused. They take advantage of every situation and twist your words. Social Services is the very definition of Psychopathic abuse.

2. Be nice, just like when you are dealing with the police. Getting upset only makes matters worse. Stick to facts and don't go into long detail about your ex-spouse. Disprove the reason for their visit based on fact.

3. While I know they are supposed to act to protect children, they don't. Workers making $25 per hour have the ability to destroy a family to the point where it is irreparable. There is zero accountability and zero recourse. This agency is the absolute worst part of the system, and the tragic part is that they actually have the ability to do so much good in this world.

4. Five false complaints of sexual abuse of grandchildren were filed against my spouse (1) and daughter (4) in three counties of our state. Police and CPS knocking at various doors, one time with one of the narcissist's minions also present. Skilled and dedicated CPS workers and police listened to us with respect and compassion, examined the documentation we had of prior false reporting (in the latter cases), and in each case concluded in our favor (unsubstantiated). By the last case, almost 2 years

ago, CPS moved to protect the children who were being gaslighted by the narcissist and his family. They were being groomed to falsely report sexual abuse. CPS worked with GAL who got the Judge to order supervised parenting time by a third party. It is never fun to have CPS involved. It scares all of us, and there is variability among the caseworkers in their training, motivation, and talent. In our cases, which involved about 20 CPS people and 8 police officers, they ALL understood, cared, and wanted to protect the children. The system worked as it should in our case. Note: If you have an unsubstantiated case with CPS make sure you request the final report and keep it in a very safe case because they are purged from CPS' records after 6 months. Our documents were the only copies available to CPS and GAL. Had we not kept them, it would have been our word against that of the narcissist's. Keeping these records is the only way one can prove a pattern of making false reports and these reports are needed by GAL and other court personnel. Because we had requested and saved our reports, the GAL understood what was going on in the current CPS report and communicated that to the Judge. Saving paper and electronic files is recommended in case it disappears or is lost in house fires, etc. We scanned ours into PDFs and keep them (daughter does and I do) on Google Docs so we can have immediate access in case of another crisis intervention. We have all of the GAL reports and Judge's orders stored electronically also.

5. Our DFS took the kids from me based on lies and manipulations, while I followed the doctor's and professional's advice on protecting our four children from their abusive father. It took me a year-and-a-half of waiting for the appeal to be completed. Finally, the 3 appellate Judges found in my favor saying I did not abuse the children, posed no future harm, found him guilty of abuse and neglect, and said that the Juvenile Court should not have taken custody. During the wait for the appeal decision, our divorce trial occurred in Family Court and he only had DFS witness's at the trial...leading to me losing full legal and physical custody of my children to their abuser. He

continues to abuse the children and myself. We are in modification, with our trial scheduled in July. I am fighting for my babies. It has been three long years of fighting and losing almost everything! I have spent all my life savings and retirement fighting for my babies! I lost the order of relief in October of last year, which we filed four months after I won my appeal. We filed for modification the very next month. Such a long legal road and each month that passes I am alienated a little more. I'm lucky to get one call a week and I only get to spend time with them when they stay at my parent's house every other weekend. The abuse, coaching, alienation and control continue! DFS made me lose my house, my job as a Daycare Director, my career, my children, my reputation, my Church family, and some friendships. Most of all, I've lost precious time with my babies. My relationship with them will never be the same. They also enabled the abuser to continue to abuse and control and lie!

Psychological Evaluations

In my case, I was not able to obtain a psychological evaluation despite our first mediator recommending one to the Commissioner and my numerous requests to the court. When inquiring about this topic with my daughters' court appointed attorney, I was told that we would need to show $8,000 before the Commissioner would recommend a Psychological Evaluation. To sum it up, our financial status – or lack thereof – prevented us from obtaining the psychological evaluation and testing.

I have been told by numerous sources that even with a test that shows positive for a Cluster B personality disorder, most Judges are not trained to understand how serious these disorders can be. Christie Brinkley's ex-husband, Peter Cook is a great example of this. Mr. Cook was diagnosed during a court-ordered psychiatric evaluation as having malignant NPD, yet even with that diagnosis, it is my belief that the courts did not act in a fashion that showed they understood the magnitude of this disorder. Mr. Cook has been allowed to harass Ms. Brinkley for years while her main goal is, and always has been, to have peace. Sadly, I don't think that she will be able to obtain peace if her ex-husband is allowed to continue his abusive tirades.

Much like custody evaluations, information for this evaluation is gathered from a variety of sources. It is important to note that determinations are not made solely on the psychological testing. Therefore, it is important to show patterns of concerning behavior. Sadly, even trained professionals can be romanced by the charming narcissist. I cannot begin to count the number of psychologists and psychiatrists who have turned to my forum for advice and support in the aftermath of a relationship with an individual suffering from NPD. No one is immune, and the burden is on you to show the true colors of the person that you are dealing with.

Advice from the Battlefield:

1. My advice would be to just cover the main themes that concern you about your narcissist and his/her parenting of your child(ren). Make a few notes so you don't forget which items are most important to you. The true narcissist will inevitably make their sessions about how you have done them wrong, and will have little focus on the child(ren). They will, if given the time, self-destruct in this process because they can't help but let their true colors show. I believe those with accompanying Cluster B personality disorders will be the ones to truly be found to have issues.

2. Make sure you know if the MMPI-2 is part of the testing. True Narcissists won't be able to get results that aren't reflective of their personality because they believe their own invincibility. As such, they are convinced they are bound to come across the way they want. The lie scale will help show that. Research your (hopefully) court-appointed psychologist. Hopefully they are a forensic psychologist and they are skilled at these types of evaluations. The more well-respected the psychologist in your family court system, the better. Ask your attorney or guardian ad litem which psychologist the court respects most and make attempts at getting the opposing side to agree to that person. If you have a good GAL, let him/her make the recommendation based on who they know has high professional integrity and is truly an expert in their field.

3. Don't study for the evaluation. There is nothing to pass. You

just need to be yourself. Be honest, and take ownership of your own issues, unlike the narcissist in your life. I looked into this a lot because I wanted to prove that my ex had a personality disorder (PD). I have read multiple sources and talked to three attorneys that said court evaluators, whether psych or custody, are not going to stick their neck out and "label" someone with a PD. They might mention patterns of violence, etc but never actually DIAGNOSE... Then what's the point?! Some wishy-washy opinion for $10,000. No thanks.

4. We both had a psych evaluation, recommended by the GAL. Probably because I requested the ex to have one -- I should've read this site before my court experience, not after! His evaluation said he probably had anger and temper issues, but then played those down as unimportant-sounding. Mine said PTSD-type stuff, consistent with his temper. Both of us were sort of high on the Lie scale. I was really surprised because I was so sure I'd been completely honest -- So sure that I researched it (I researched all the info in our test results) and saw that the Lie scale is scored high if it looks like you're trying to make yourself look too good, along with the checks & balances where they compare answers to similar questions. So a priest who has actually lived a great life might score high on the Lie scale because the test thinks no one could actually BE that good. It's a known thing that certain people tend to score higher on the Lie scale: divorcing parents because they're trying to make themselves look good for court. And also people who are highly educated, intelligent and/or wealthy. This is because some of the answers, when answered truthfully by these people, make the test scorer think, "This person can't really be that smart." For example, "I think I am smarter than the average person." -- well, if you know your IQ is super high and your whole life you've been in Gifted classes, etc., then the answer to that would truthfully be "Yes." Both my ex- narcissist and I are intelligent, highly-educated people with some decent money, who are also divorcing. We took this evaluation for court -- so it's no surprise now, after I read that information, that we both scored high on the Lie scale, even though I was so sure I'd been

truthful. Our evaluations were $1,000 for each of us, plus we paid half each for our daughter to have one. Her results also verified her dad's temper. Nothing was ever mentioned about that in court, though. That's what is most frustrating, and I see others saying the same thing: when evidence that we spend time gathering, presenting, paying for experts, etc., is just ignored!

5. My ex and I both had them, and even though his showed definite violence and interpersonal problems and mine showed peace-keeping traits, the Judge threw it all out and ignored it. He said quote unquote, "we all have a little something on our psych evals, so I'm going to disregard" .... Then my children went on to be abused and have ended up with PTSD from the split custody with their father. After all was said and done, I had to 'clean up the mess' - it took me a year or more of extreme parenting to get them back on track.

6. Custody evaluators use a variety of tests to choose from such as The Millon Clinical MultiAxial Inventory (MCMMI-3), Bricklin Perceptual Scales (BPS), Thematic Apperception Test (TAT) and the Ackerman-Schoendorf Scales for Parent Evaluation of Custody (ASPECT). The vast majority of the time, the test utilized is only one portion of the evaluation. Similar to a regular custody evaluation, the evaluator relies heavily upon interviews with the parents, children and other individuals who have first-hand knowledge of the family and the situation. This includes teachers, nannies, childcare providers, etc. The important thing to remember is that the final decision is in the hands of the court and not the evaluator.

7. This is what I found to work best: Tape record all meetings with evaluator and have them transcribed. Have a 3rd party "support person" at the home inspection if allowed – my house was immaculate and that was used against me as being hyper-vigilant. Little did the evaluator know the house keeper was there and her scheduled day just happened to be on the day he was scheduled. Ask for qualifications and check the qualifications in addition to having your attorney qualify them on the stand. Find out if this is a full evaluation or a fast-track

evaluation (Google 730 evaluations for more information). I also recommend using an attorney from out of town – they cost more but they do not care if they step on toes which, for locals, would generally mean lack of referrals. Gather evidence of DUIs or crimes committed by relatives (of ex spouse) who will be around the child and present it by fax so evaluator can't say in court he didn't get it. Consider a PI to document alcohol abuse, partying, etc. to show the environment that your child will be subjected to. If the testing comes out suspicious, go to two other experts and be tested so the evaluator can be challenged on the stand if the tests don't match.

Minor's Counsel

The goal of a Minor's Counsel or GAL (Guardian Ad Litem) is to represent the best interests of the child and to form an unbiased opinion of what that is to present to the court. The overall goal is not to take sides with either parent but to get to the bottom of the issues plaguing custody battles. Generally, Minor's Counsel will interview teachers, nannies, church leaders, childcare providers and counselors as well as both parents and the children.

I began asking for Minor's Counsel very early on in our custody battle when I sensed that the court did not have the time to invest in our case. When the Commissioner began to be overwhelmed with the chaos that was our divorce, he handed our case over to the only attorney who happened to be standing in the courtroom at that moment. That man had no idea what assignment was landing in his lap. Many would say he was in the wrong place at the wrong time.

The gentleman who was appointed to represent my daughters is a very well-known attorney in our area. He is known as "the one" to retain if you want to win and his rates reflect his reputation at $450 per hour. Luckily, we were given a reduced rate of $100 per hour which still adds up over a two year period when you are dealing with a case like ours.

Unfortunately, Minor's Counsel was not prepared for Seth and it took two years for him to finally see the full picture. I believe that, originally, he saw us as a typical high-conflict divorce and had high hopes that the tensions would settle with time. He repeatedly gave Seth the benefit of the doubt and, while he seemed annoyed with him on multiple occasions, he held out hope that Seth would get himself together and be the dad that he claimed to be.

One thing that remained consistently confusing to me was the way the Commissioner seemed to rule once Minor's Counsel came onboard. In my naïve but logical thinking, I assumed that the attorney was appointed to get to the bottom of the issues at hand. I assumed that Minor's Counsel's recommendation would be treated as gold. In actuality, it was quite the opposite. If Minor's Counsel recommended supervised visits then the Commissioner ordered unsupervised visits. If Minor's Counsel recommended unsupervised visits then the Commissioner would grant supervised visits. I was often left wondering why I was paying $100 an hour for an opinion that didn't seem to matter.

Over the past few years, I have listened to a multitude of good and bad experiences as they relate to Minor's Counsel. While the majority of stories I've heard are not favorable, there are some attorneys who are intent on doing what is best for the children.

Advice from the Battlefield:

1. The things I wish I knew were this: what was professionally expected of a GAL; what the qualifications were to be a GAL; what qualifications my GAL actually had; the process for airing concerns about the GAL's conduct and whether or not they were affiliated with any father's rights groups.

2. First thing to remember about your minor's counsel is that if you act nervous, the children can pick up on that and pass it on in their interview with him or her. I always told my children that she was there to help and all they needed to do was be honest.

3. My ex-wife repeatedly coached my children on what to say before meeting with our GAL. This was going on for weeks prior to our first appointment. I made sure to email our GAL and let her know that I was concerned about the children being prepped. I told the children that their job was to answer all questions truthfully and that adults were not allowed to tell them what to say. Thankfully, the GAL was well versed and

asked the children whether anyone had told them what to say. They were honest about everything and it showed that my ex-wife was very conniving and had things to hide.

4. I prepared a list of concerns prior to the first meeting and answered all questions presented to me in a truthful manner. I provided a timeline of events along with a list of character witnesses and declarations from my pastor, child's teacher, Girl Scout's leader, babysitters and a separate list of individuals who had witnessed disturbing behavior or incidents during or after our marriage.

5. Just like in court, it is important to be calm, factual, and void of emotions. Let them know that your goal is to encourage the child's relationship with the other parent, however, your goal is to also ensure that it is a safe, healthy environment. Explain to the children that this person is part of a team who will work to decide what is best for him/her. This person is a friend and, like with any friend, honesty is very important.

Appeals

While I have never personally appealed a court ruling, I know many who have, and the first word that comes to my mind when I hear the word is, "expensive." There were multiple times when I felt like appealing decisions but I felt as though it would be an uphill battle and so I chose to stay the course and continue documenting in an effort to establish patterns. In my case, I knew it was a matter of time before Seth hung himself. My greatest fear was that waiting would come at the expense of my children's safety and well-being. In those fearful moments, I had to lean heavily on my faith.

I was recently contacted by a One Mom's Battle (OMB) Warrior Mom who was happy to share her thoughts based on experience.

> *An appeal is VERY expensive (on average: $30,000). I felt that I had no choice but to appeal, being that in my order it was written that in the event we returned to court, I would most likely lose custody.*

> *What I didn't realize was that the job of the Appellate Court is*

essentially to find a way to maintain the existing ruling, so it is an uphill battle. In addition to this, in New York, transcripts are also very expensive. ($3-$4/page - and one minute of testimony is typically a page).

I was fortunate enough to be able to get a Home Equity Loan for $20,000. I was also able to find an appeals attorney that was willing to do my appeal for $15,000 and the transcripts came to $4,000. Of that expense, the $4,000 for the transcripts was worth every penny. It was the first time in nearly ten years that I could see the lies and manipulation in black-and-white.

Yet, I would never recommend appealing. I would have been much better off spending two years documenting everything and brining my case back to court. Also, I met with multiple politicians, and one congresswoman was able to help get the person who ruled on my case terminated. But, had that not happened, I later learned that I could petition to be heard by a different Judge. In my opinion: Rarely is an appeal worth it -- and if anything, it further justifies a bad decision.

Advice from the Battlefield:

1. There is SO much about the Appellate Court that leads me to believe that it is just one more level of corruption.

2. I did a De Novo, which is very similar to the appeal process. The Judge was looking for something wrong with the hearing instead of looking to overturn the decision. It was a very expensive hearing and I could have made much better use of the money spent.

3. My advice for anyone considering an Appeal would be this: If your Divorce Attorney whispers to you during your Final Hearing "We're going to appeal," know that you have to get every bit of evidence that you want heard to be read on record during that Hearing. Unless it's part of the final hearing, it won't be addressed during the appeal. Your attorney has probably already noted several instances that the Judge has violated your legal rights or s/he wouldn't have brought it up.

- Hire an Appeals Attorney for that part of the battle.

- Try to see if your Appeals Attorney will agree to a price cap for the entire procedure.

- Getting a transcript of the judgment that is being appealed is worth the cost.

- Remember that you are appealing the Judge's actions and nothing else.

- If you win the appeal and the unfair decision isn't overturned, you've just won the opportunity to retry the final hearing. In my case that will be in front of the same Judge that caused the need for an appeal.

My experience has been that everything that can be said, has been said, which makes the appeal less stressful than the hearings. I'm glad I have an agreed upon price cap and an attorney with a good track record against this particular Judge. I'm also glad I'm not arguing against a custody decision. Those don't get overturned very often. If I win the appeal and get a second final hearing with another verdict contrary to Family Law statutes, I will have to appeal again. After the second appeal the verdict can be overturned at the State Court level. Fingers crossed that legal statutes are adhered to and nobody's personal prejudices are a part of the equation...this time.

4. Appealing a custody decision does not seem worth the money. These decisions are rarely overturned due to the fact that so much depends on what a Judge "assessed and observed" regarding the demeanor of the parties. As we know, narcissists can fool anyone. But appealing judgments regarding the division of property are much more straight-forward, from what I understand.

5. I appealed our child support. The ex had not and did not want to pay. He deliberately worked under the table to avoid having to pay. I filed and asked for support to be based on income potential based on previous income. The ex didn't come to court that day, but the support unit testified that the ex contacted them to confirm the date, showing that he was well aware. My support was increased from a ridiculously low $90 a month to something more reasonable. He has appealed to both the court and the recovery unit on numerous occasions, but to no avail. I did this pro se. This is the only appeal we have had, since I was told that appealing our custody and visitation wouldn't be worth the fight and the amount of money that it would cost.

Child Support

My child support is a topic that is laughable at best because while Seth makes six-figures when working, he is unable to hold a job for more than four months at a time. After each job loss, it takes child support services about two months to garnish his wages and by the time they are regularly collecting child support, he loses his job and the cycle starts all over again. Currently, Seth's child support arrears sits at just over $40,000.00. To date, he has never lost his driver's license nor has he had his passport revoked, which still baffles me.

My goal from the very beginning was to get to a place where I was not dependent on Seth for child support. With each job that Seth lost, my world would come crashing down. I often found myself scrambling to pay for childcare costs, groceries and basic necessities. Each job loss and missed child support payment resulted in an email to Seth and conflict quickly ensued each time. Seth thrived off berating me and he loved to remind me that I was riding his coattails and worthless without his money.

I hated that Seth had any degree of control over my life or my emotions. Every two weeks, I was dependent upon the deposit into my checking account. If the payment was a day or two late, I immediately assumed that he had lost his job and anxiety crept in. I was working very hard to get on my feet and out from under Seth's financial wrath.

In 2009, shortly after my marriage ended, my business which was like a child to me also ended. I had been an entrepreneur since I was 19 years old and found myself in need of a job for the first time in many years. I landed an entry-level position with an advertising agency which thrilled me because I had always loved PR and marketing. Over a four year period of time, I worked my way up in my career and regained my independence.

During those years, things were not easy. Humbling would be an understatement. I didn't have a bed to sleep in and gratefully accepted an old, donated bed that my friends affectionately deemed the "1970's porn star poster bed." It was ugly and horrendous. I lived in a shoebox apartment for over six months that was perfect for a college student or a woman with 32 cats. Let's just say it was less than nice. On Thursday mornings, I would email our church receptionist with my grocery "wish list" and she would be ready at 5pm to load the bags into my car so that I didn't have to personally visit the food bank. My car was scheduled to be repossessed and I sold my wedding ring, which was valued at $11,000, for $3,000. That small chunk of money felt like a million dollars and allowed me to put down a deposit on a car with 120,000 miles on it.

Looking back, it was by far the craziest time that I can remember. I was juggling every aspect of my life and holding on by a thread. While there were many times that I cried myself to sleep, I knew that the financial stress I was experiencing was worth it just to be free. My 600-square foot cat-lady apartment had something that my 4,300 square foot luxury home lacked: love and freedom.

Five years after my nightmare first began, I am proud to say that I am finally in the place that I dreamed about when I first started this process. While child support payments provide my daughters with nicer clothing, extracurricular activities and a better life, we are no longer dependent on Seth. If the child support check comes, fabulous. If Seth loses his job and the unemployment cycle starts, it is frustrating, but it doesn't control my world. I allow Child Support Services to handle the situation and I am able to step back and allow them to do their job. Seth doesn't control me or any aspect of my life, and that is a feeling that I will never tire of. He is welcomed to obsess about money day in and day out but he will never again pull my puppet strings. Let freedom ring!

Advice from the Battlefield:

1. It's important to understand that, for the majority of narcissists, money is more important than to them than their children. Not only do they want to keep "their" money, but they especially want to keep it from going to you (the ex-spouse). Therefore, children are just a bargaining chip in a narcissist's effort to keep their money. If keeping the kids with him means paying you less money, then that's what they do. It has nothing to do with what's best for the kids, or you or even him. It's about the money. So, if you give up the money, you get the kids. That is an extremely painful concept for soon to be ex-spouses to come to grips with, but if you start your journey understanding this, you will be better off in the long run.

2. The best approach to child support from a narcissist is to never expect any and to budget without child support income. Appreciate it if it arrives, but never become dependent upon it for survival as the narcissist is a master at turning it into a noose around your neck. Ours worked under the table for years, lied about it in court and said he was attending college (another lie), but there was never any accountability by Judge for the proven lies. He was trying to break me and would offer to take the children if we could not provide for them. Finally, he got tired of living that way (we outlasted him). He got a real job and, when we found out, we were able to have his wages garnished. Of course, with the extra income he hired an attorney and waged custody battle meaning the child support was greatly overcome by attorney fees. Vicious cycle.

3. My ex-husband LOVES the control that comes with child support. It is how I pay my rent. We recently got into a disagreement, just days before Christmas and days before rent was due, and the first words out of his mouth were, "Good luck coming up with rent now since you want to try and fight with me." I am on my way to becoming financially independent and I cannot wait until I am. Any last little bit of control he has will finally be gone.

4. Given the narcissist's propensity to lie, get as much proof of their earnings as possible. My ex-narcissist was found to be "voluntarily underemployed" by the Judge - this is important, because I knew he was purposely NOT working at the time of the trial in order to appear too "poor" for child support. Additionally, we got the Judge to IMPUTE his income...this is a judgment call about what the narcissist is capable of earning as opposed to what he is actually earning at the time of the trial. The narcissist's income was imputed to be high based on his past earnings (which I proved with narcissist's pay stubs and old emails where he used to brag to me about how much he earned – from early in our relationship when he was trying to impress me) as well as his resume, which showed all his college degrees and past high-level jobs. So...get your PROOF of your

narcissist's earnings and try to get the Judge to IMPUTE his worth if he is purposely trying to look "poor". When your ex-narcissist fails to pay CS after having been ordered to do so, be prepared to file a motion to hold him in contempt of court for violation of court orders

5. What's worse than the narcissist's attitude toward child support is the way the Attorney General's office and/or court system handles it. In Texas, they send out a letter every three years stating you can have it reviewed. They don't tell you that it takes at least another three years to get anything done. Plus, if a parent is paying something, even $25, they won't go after them. They simply think "well, at least he is paying something". Have a narcissist that is self employed and it's next to impossible to get any money through garnishments or other means. Add a narcissist that avoids being served like the plague and you have a recipe for nothing getting done EVER. I mean, the AG's office isn't going to pay for a private server, so they'll just try every now and then to serve him only he won't answer his door. Above the law - that's where they live. I never knew you didn't have to answer the door to law enforcement until I met the narcissist.

"You may encounter many defeats, but you must not be defeated. In fact, it may be necessary to encounter the defeats, so you can know who you are, what you can rise from, how you can still come out of it."

-Maya Angelou

<u>THE NARC DECODER</u>

While divorce is generally riddled with varying degrees of conflict, divorcing a narcissist will take the conflict to heights that few can comprehend. People who suffer from Narcissistic Personality Disorder are both incapable of compromise and they are overcome by the need to win. This is obviously a bad combination in divorce court.

The rule when dealing with a narcissist is simple but critical: no engagement. Similar to a drug addict, narcissists need to derive emotion from their victims. If a drug dealer stopped selling drugs then the addicts would find a new supplier and stop returning. Stop giving them what they want, which is your time, energy and emotions.

While co-parenting requires communication, it needs to be limited and entirely free of emotions. Communicating with a narcissist is like running on a hamster wheel. You can wear yourself out to the point of exhaustion, yet you never left point A. Picture the exhausted little hamster (insert your face on tiny little furry body) every time you feel compelled to respond to an email.

Narcissists thrive on evoking both reactions and emotions from their victims. In the beginning stages of my divorce, I would dread opening my email account and cringe at the mere sound of a text message. Both means of communication became avenues for attacks or narcissistic rages. As a narcissist who was set on winning and hurting me at all costs, my ex-husband thrived on creating unrest. As I became educated on this personality disorder, I began to repair the cracks in my foundation and I became increasingly empowered as I healed through education. I began to take the power back. I chose to be a survivor versus a victim.

Over time, I've learned how to communicate in a way that allows me to maintain my sanity. Communication with a narcissist is best described as "crazy making" because narcissists are known to reinvent reality to suite their personal agenda. Leading psychiatrist Dr. Carole Lieberman, M.D. weighed in on the topic to further explain the mindset of a narcissist: *"Since narcissists believe that the world revolves around them, or that it should, they think they can reinvent reality and no one should question them. Even though they know that what they're writing or saying is stretching the truth, they think that they are so clever about it that they will fool the recipient into going along with them."*

I now see through the emails and instead of angst, I felt pity. I started to re-write the emails to reveal the true nature of my ex-husband's words. I took it a step further and added humor to the situation by creating something that I affectionately refer to as the "Narc Decoder". This device is patent pending and can analyze and decipher the most cryptic and bizarre narcissistic emails.

In an effort to demonstrate how the Narc Decoder works, I will insert the following email that I received this year:

> *Tina- None of the men in my family have committed an act of harm towards a woman. It's just delusional that you have such fear of me. I have previously thought about having the exchange at the Police Department. The police department is a scary setting for the children and there is no reason for it. When I was a kid Police made me nervous. You think after you've dragged me to court for three years over nonsense and exaggerations, I would risk yelling at you or harming you, it's just preposterous, Tina. I am not going to do anything to hurt you. I will compromise and agree to meet you at the park. - Seth*

In the past I would have sat down and tried to reason with my ex-husband by citing examples of his behavior that caused me concern. I would have explained why I felt more comfortable meeting at the police station and reminded him why we've had so many court dates. I would have spent entirely too much time and energy attempting to create sanity out of insanity. Sometimes I want to travel backwards in time and shake some sense into the old me.

"Snap, fizzle, pop" and out comes the de-coded email:

> *Tina- I have not yet committed an act of harm towards a woman, but I am starting to worry about the fact that three different women have now testified that they live in fear due to my instability, stalking and passive-aggressive threats. Since I have had multiple run-ins with law enforcement over the past ten years, police make me nervous and cause increased anxiety. I would prefer that we do not meet near a police station. Thank you, Seth*

Suggested response: *"We will see you at the court-ordered meeting location at 9am.Thank you, Tina"*

Over the years, I've spent a lot of time processing emails from members of the One Mom's Battle website. Teaching the men and women of OMB how to read these emails on their own has been a gratifying experience. In essence, it helps teach people how to regain their power in the aftermath of a narcissist. The following is an email submitted by a warrior mom from One

Mom's Battle:

> *"I wish I had a mirror to have you see how you come across in your
> presentation. Maybe there would be a slim possibility you could see
> how angry, inflexible, demanding a person that you are. Why would
> anybody want to work anything out with you! You do not know the
> first thing about being accommodating, understanding, or
> professional for any matters. So you run to your attorney to find
> solutions. Besides, the selfishness that is your true self. All you
> know to do is fight, fight, fight. How very sad because one day it
> will have an effect on your existence if you keep it up. Find a better
> way to channel your anger that life is not fair for you or you may
> face the consequences.*
>
> *Soon there will be no need to consider "the Family Wizard" for
> communication because I will rarely have any contact with you
> except to discuss logistics. So it is totally off the table. Period.*
>
> *I, too, have plans for myself and our daughter, so you are not
> privileged in setting what weekend day we do the exchange. In fact,
> as I said before, I gave you 18 months of many episodes of
> flexibility and that will not be easy to get anymore. You cannot
> make Sundays a unilateral condition for hours that were decided by
> my employer, speaking of being unilateral. Life does not care what
> you think!*
>
> *I will not waste anymore of my valuable time today with your
> expressions of whining and discontent."*

"Snap, fizzle, pop" and out comes the de-coded email:

> *"I wish I had a mirror right now so that I could see myself. I could
> spend hours staring into my own eyes. Have I told you lately how
> angry I am at the loss of power since our marriage ended? Yes, I'm
> angry, inflexible and demanding, and all of those feelings have
> escalated tremendously since I can no longer control you. Damn
> you. I refuse to compromise or work anything out with you – it's my
> way or the highway. Didn't you read the fine print on the pre-nup?
> I do not know the first thing about being accommodating,
> understanding or professional but instead of taking ownership for*

my own shortcomings; I am going to project my faults on to you. Heck, it's always worked in the past.

I hate that you have an attorney to turn to for advice – why can't you just let me continue to control and manipulate you?! It's quite infuriating. I love to fight, fight, fight. This constant drama feeds me because I know that it affects you. I LOVE to affect you. Speaking of love, did you know that I am actually incapable of that? Thank God I am so manipulative because that's how I am able to fool women just like I fooled you. Have you seen my mirror lately? Aren't you supposed to keep track of my things?

Our Family Wizard? Are you joking? Do you really think that I want my words and actions to be monitored? Ha! I want access to you by all means possible – text, phone, email, in person and while shouting from the rooftops. You want ME to agree to something that YOU think is a good idea? Ha! Did I mention that I am a control freak and a program like that would not work well for me? The only way that I will agree to use that program is if it somehow becomes my idea. I will be sure to request that YOU be required to use it while we are in front of the Judge because doing so will play into my claim that you are harassing me and suggest the program will put an end to your persistent abuse. By the way, have you ever heard of a program called, "Our Family Wizard?" I happened to find it online yesterday and I think we should begin to use it. I am tired of the constant harassment from you.

You want me to be flexible on times for visitation. I'm sorry but that is a one-way street. You must adhere to the court order word for word, however, I will let you know when I need you to bend. Oh, by the way, next weekend doesn't work well for me as I have a lunch date. I'll need you to take our daughter for a few extra hours.

Have I mentioned how valuable my time is? I should get paid to just be awake and breathing. Now that I've thoroughly fed my sick, deranged ego, I am going to sit here and gloat knowing that you are on the receiving end of my latest attack. I'm going to envision you breaking down crying because that is like a high to me."

Suggested response: *"We will plan to adhere to the visitation schedule as it is written. Thank you, Angie"*

Nothing more. Nothing less. Polite and business-like. From this point on, adhere to the schedule as it is written. A simple request opens you up for an attack such as the one above. Sticking to the court-ordered schedule goes both ways and with a narcissist, it is imperative that you do not deviate from the court order.

Christie Brinkley's divorce has made the spotlight over the years because her ex-husband, Peter Cook, thrives on chaos like most people with personality disorders. In 2008, Dr. Stephen Herman, a court-appointed psychiatrist affiliated with Weill Medical College of Cornell University, testified that Peter was a narcissist in an effort to explain Cook's behaviors to the court. Peter Cook regularly demonstrates a trademark of NPD which is most often shown post-divorce; he cannot handle the thought of his ex-wife thriving or being happy without him. Christie's happiness is poison to Peter Cook and he demonstrates this through regular and greatly predictable temper tantrums.

Dr. Carole Lieberman, M.D., psychiatrist and author of "Bad Girls: Why Men Love Them & How Good Girls Can Learn Their Secrets" provided insight into Peter Cook's behavior:

> *"Narcissists create a world for themselves in which they are the center. They believe their own view of the world they've created. It is clear from Peter Cook's letter that he believes what he is saying. But, much of it is his own projection. He berates Christie for not getting over the divorce and continuing to focus on and belittle him, when it's the other way around. He, apparently, hasn't gotten over the divorce and jumps at any opportunity to get back in the media to continue to criticize Christie, by way of their marriage and divorce.*
>
> *Peter is of an age where he's worrying about 'still being sexy at (almost) 60', so this article is touching on a very sensitive nerve for him. He cheated with an 18-year-old, and he's wondering, or perhaps already doubts, that 18-year-olds will still find him sexy. So, to see Christie looking fabulous, on the top of her game, and on the cover of a magazine, feels like a slap in the face which only*

highlights his inadequacies. It's not really anything she said, it's how she's come out on top."

Peter Cook, in an effort to receive media attention submitted the following open letter to Christie Brinkley via the online website, Radar Online:

Christie, over the last 8 years I have taken a lot of hits by way of your gross exaggerations, revisionist history, and self-serving dishonesty, but nothing could be more egregious than this incontrovertible lie. I let you get away with a lot for the sake our children. When you initially filed for divorce and you attempted to prejudice opinion of me by falsely accusing me of EVER being inappropriate with Sailor was the death knell for me as far as you were concerned. That was the day I took my wedding ring off.

You know I could not love or care for my children more, and that I have NEVER raised my hand to ANYONE, or surely you would not have encourage my adoption of Jack 3-years after we married. That you could so blatantly lie about such a sacred trust to position yourself as a victim once again is disgraceful. I didn't think you could get any lower in you endeavors to stay relevant in the media than through your relentless trashing of the father of your children, and I don't care about you or what motivates you to now perpetuate this horrific lie, and then to have your PR team work so diligently to see it is perpetuated throughout all possible media outlets... but I insist that you immediately demand that they work as thoroughly and dilligently to issue YOUR PERSONAL public correction/retraction and demand this libelous content be wiped from the media, immediately.

Nothing could be more upsetting than being falsely accused of being abusive to one's children, particularly given the irony that the greatest abuse these children have endured is your insistence on publicizing our trial, our divorce these many years later, and making them suffer your need for attention at any and all cost:

'Brinkley won a large settlement, especially after revelation of Cook's heavy hand on the three children.' In PEOPLE Magazine you state your '50's weren't easy' because you '...went through a

*miserable divorce (from architect Peter Cook) while trying TO BE
A PILLAR FOR MY KIDS…'*

*There is nothing about YOU FIGHTING and CAMPAIGNING to
see our divorce proceedings were publicized, making our private
lives media fodder for our children to have to endure for GOOGLE
eternity, making false and dishonest statements about the father of
your children and making every effort to alienate the children from
their father that qualifies you as being a "pillar" for our
children!"* –Peter Cook

"Snap, fizzle, pop" and out comes the de-coded email:

Christie,

*I am foaming at the mouth over the fact that you are receiving press
(again) and that you so happy. Please sit tight as I project my own
behaviors, gross exaggerations and self-serving dishonesty onto
you. I may even minimize my past and current behavior, which is
what narcissists generally do!*

*The first day that I took my wedding ring off was the day I met 15-
year old Diana Bianchi in a toy store. Many believed that I was
there under the guise of a doting father but you and I both know
why I was there. How dare the media pick up on this! The only
reason that this even made the news is because you are a celebrity.
The more that I think about it, my affair was your fault!*

*I am still quite furious that you didn't insist on our divorce being
kept sealed and private. Regardless of the fact that all divorces in
New York are public record, I am above common-folk and feel
entitled to keep my $3,000 per month porn habit under wraps. Just
think how deceitful I could have been while "accidentally" feeding
the media my lies. With a sealed divorce, there would have been no
way for the media to verify any of it. Why can't you just start doing
what I say?*

*I am incredibly bitter that the media is still interested in you and
that my modeling career bombed very early on. I am angry that a
major modeling agency picked you up at 60 years old. My hope is*

that you will become as ugly on the outside as I am on the inside. Someone out there needs to start believing that you are a selfish monster who is relentlessly trashing me, the father of your children. The challenging part for me is that in all these years, no one can actually find a single statement in which you've disparaged me. I am so frustrated by this and I demand that you immediately retract all of the things that you've never said about me!

As you know, I have needlessly dragged our children through the media because my narcissistic supply sits on empty the vast majority of the time. My "refuel" light starts flashing every single time you receive media attention and, as we both know, I prey on those who are uneducated on NPD so that they will report that we are feuding. By definition, it takes two people to feud however, the general population isn't that smart and they generally pool us together while the sad reality is that I feud all by myself. Peter Cook versus Peter Cook. Won't you please join in this battle?

In regards to my statement to Radar Online, "But the excuses for her behavior are dishonest, convenient and increasingly difficult to accept. She's simply using narcissism to distract from the real conversation." What we both know that I meant was this: how dare you use my diagnosis of Narcissistic Personality Disorder to explain my behavior. How dare you tell the truth! - Peter

Suggested response: Nothing, nada, zilch. There is nothing in this email that pertains to the child, visitation, etc. This gets filed in the folder titled, "Ignore."

When processing your own emails through the Narc Decoder, it is helpful to picture a mentally unstable 6-year old child sitting behind a computer and laughing an evil laugh. It is important to also remember that while the narcissist appears to be extremely self-confident, they are a bottomless pits of insecurities. Do not be their supplier of emotions – that is no longer your job!

"No one can make your feel inferior without your permission." - Eleanor Roosevelt

CHILDREN

Seth and I spent four years of our daughter's young lives in a full-blown war. When we separated, Piper was only four years old and Sarah was only two years old. They are now nine years old and seven years old respectively. During the battle, I prayed for my children to grow up quickly. In my mind, the older they were, the better equipped they were to face whatever Seth threw their way. Childhood is a time to enjoy and cherish however, anyone who has divorced a narcissist can relate to my feelings and angst.

It has been eight months since we've seen Seth although he still calls by phone once per week. Each week for eight months he tells the girls that he misses them and wants to see them. Sometimes, he tries to rope them in emotionally by saying things like, "We will need to figure out a way to see each other soon." Piper usually rolls her eyes because she knows all he has to do is fill out a packet of paperwork. Last week, one of Piper's friends saw a photo of Seth in her bedroom and commented that Seth was handsome. I heard Piper say, "Well, he's *not* handsome on the inside!" Out of the mouths of babes.

Day by day, our lives are returning to normal. Instead of wanting to fast-forward through my daughters' childhood, I am now wishing I could push the "pause" button. I am living in the moment and enjoying the peace. When reflecting, I feel sad that NPD stole such a large piece of Piper and Sarah's childhood.

The ups and downs of sharing custody with a narcissist is best described as a living hell. As the healthy parent, you live in fear that anything you do will be used against you. You watch in painful agony as your innocent children are manipulated, bullied and coerced. In any other situation (playground bullies, etc), you would have the full authority to teach your children that manipulating and bullying are not acceptable behaviors. You would teach your children to speak up and set boundaries yet if you teach them these lessons in relation to their narcissistic parent, the narcissist will claim alienation and you risk losing your children. The courts need to wake up and become educated on high-conflict personalities because the anti-bullying campaigns need to happen in the home as well as on the playground.

Co-Parenting

There is no such thing as co-parenting with a Narcissist. In the beginning of our divorce, and being a person who hates conflict, I envisioned Seth and I working together to ensure that the girls came first at all times. Our original nesting agreement was set up with that goal in mind. A nesting agreement essentially allows the children to stay in one home and the parents rotate in and out of the home. I didn't care how uncomfortable the situation was for me, my objective was to make sure that the girls were happy, secure and thriving at all times.

Sadly, our nesting agreement was very short-lived because…well, because Seth is a Narcissist! When you are dealing with a high-conflict individual, nesting agreements will not work, and neither will most attempts at co-parenting unless, of course, the agreement is designed to please the Narcissist – who couldn't care less about what is best for the children. The first step is to accept the sad reality that any traditional approach to co-parenting is going to be fruitless when the other parent suffers from a personality disorder.

Drama to a narcissist is like spinach to Popeye. The narcissist receives his daily vampire feed from conflict and, therefore, it is your job to maintain a peaceful environment and not get sucked into his trap. Do not engage unless it is absolutely imperative and involves the children.

Paula Lovgren, a mother and freelance writer, shared what may be the very best advice that I have encountered on parenting with a high conflict individual:

> *"To parent your children with a narcissistic parent, very little, if any, of the traditional divorce/parenting advice is going to apply. Co-parenting? Not likely. Your number one job as the non-narcissistic parent is to reduce conflict. You have to, because he won't. The narcissistic parent thrives on drama he creates because it provides him with narcissistic supply. He will take any form of supply he can get, even if it's negative. Don't engage with him. Reducing conflict with him is the best way to protect your children from the narcissist's behavior.*
>
> *How can you do this? The following steps are pretty easy in theory, but as anyone dealing with a narcissistic knows, nothing is easy. The narcissist's behavior may escalate as he realizes you are*

disengaging with him. That can be scary for you. Stand your ground. In time, hopefully, when the narcissist realizes that he's not getting any supply, he'll move on to other sources leaving you and your children in relative peace.

1. No face-to-face or phone conversations

The best way for the narcissistic to lie, manipulate and abuse is in conversations either on the phone or in person. It's not necessary to put yourself in this position. Your job as a parent is to communicate important information about your children to the other parent. Communicating means to convey information, make known, reveal clearly. Nowhere in the definition of communicate does it mention talking.

Fortunately, we now have at our disposal a myriad of ways to communicate. Unfortunately, this has also led us (and in turn, our narcissistic abusers) to believe that we must be available at all times, to all people. Even if you are parenting with a former spouse, it's not necessary for them to every phone number, email address or social media contact. In fact, if you're dealing with a narcissist, they should not. One phone number to contact the kids, one email address to contact you and an emergency contact should they need to get a hold of you on short notice is all they need.

I suggest setting up a free web-based email account that can be accessed from any computer to be used only for communicating with the N parent. This is the only email address for you he should have access to. Sure, he may continue to rant, name call, threaten and otherwise try to bait you. Now you have it all in writing in one place. If he wants to put his bad behavior in black and white, well, good for you. Now you have a record and concrete evidence of his nasty behavior. You also have all agreements, schedule changes, and any other pertinent information in writing. That's communication.

If you can have a separate phone for the kids, do it, even if it's a cell phone that stays in the home and travels with you and the children on trips. The narcissistic does not need a personal phone number for you regardless of what he may think. He's abused the privilege. There are many free texting apps, if you have a smartphone, where he can still text you in emergencies without having your personal number. If he abuses this privilege, block him. You can also have a family member or close friend be the emergency contact who will then contact you in rare circumstances.

2. Have an iron-clad divorce decree

Get visitation schedules, holidays, phone calls, activities, pick-up/drop-off times and places and anything else that you see as potentially being a problem between you and the other parent explicitly written out in the divorce decree or marital termination agreement. Try to leave as little as possible open to negotiation after the divorce is final.

The divorce decree is your shield. At first, it may seem constraining because you, too, will have to abide by those agreements. However, in the long run, it will be easier and less stressful than trying to negotiate with an unreliable and unreasonable person. In addition, when you follow the decree as it's written, anything he does in opposition to that is highlighted. Don't argue with him. Let him hang himself with his own behavior. Just more good documentation for you.

3. Get healthy.

You have come out of an abusive relationship and now you need to be as emotionally healthy as possible for your children. As easy as it is to write a list of what to do when divorcing a narcissist, every single one of us knows that it's anything but easy. It takes time, healing and a really good support system to help you disengage from a narcissist and his crazy-making ways.

Seek counseling or a support group that focuses on abusive/narcissistic relationships. The narcissist isn't likely to change. Having a support system will help you hold your boundaries with him and focus your attention on yourself and your children instead of his antics. He's had enough of your time and attention. Don't give him any more.

4. Validate and empower your children.

If reducing conflict with the other parent is your number one job, a close second is validating and empowering your children. You know how the narcissist operates and he will treat his children no differently. You can't change him and unless there is verifiable, concrete evidence that his children aren't safe with him (physical/sexual abuse, drug/alcohol addiction) your children will most likely have to spend time with him.

As much as we want to, we really can't protect our children from the narcissist's insidious behavior. As much as we believe it's better for them to be shielded from it, they deserve to spend time with their other parent. Regardless of his behavior, your children love their other parent. They might not always like him, but they do love him and they do deserve the right to make up their own mind about their parent. I'm not going to lie, this is really hard. Really, really hard. As a therapist once said to me, "you have to let your children make up their own mind or they may turn their anger on you for cutting their parent out of their life. They won't understand why, only that you ruined that relationship." Ouch! Better to let the narcissist do it himself.

What you can do is be your children's number one support system and sounding board. Validate, validate, validate! You know how the narcissist lies, manipulates and distorts reality. It's not bashing your former spouse to validate your child's feelings or to say that certain behavior is not okay. They need to be supported in their own reality because they already know something is wrong. They are looking for a mooring place in the rocky sea the narcissist creates. Use neutral statements, like "I'm sorry that happened," "I'll bet that feels bad," or just simply "Ouch." Above all, let your children know that their parent's behavior and treatment of them has nothing whatsoever do with them.

Lastly, don't take it all on yourself. Children can benefit greatly from having a therapist who specializes in working with children. Play therapy is wonderful. Children don't even know that they are in "therapy." They just know they have a really good friend who listens to them. Having a neutral third party validate the same things that you are takes away the "mom versus dad" mentality. They will begin to trust their own thoughts and feelings about the situation and to realize on their own that their parent's behavior is not okay.

Reducing conflict with a narcissistic parent will often feel like an ineffective battle at best and additional fuel to the abusive fire at worst. At the outset, the narcissist's behavior is likely to escalate as he realizes he's losing control. Stay strong and keep your focus on yourself and your children, not the narcissist's antics. Hopefully, when he realizes he's playing his games with himself, he'll get the message and find his narcissistic supply elsewhere."

Advice from the Battlefield:

1. The day I got a Judge to acknowledge that parallel parenting was the only thing that was going to work was a huge sigh of relief. Most social workers, case workers, GALs and mediators are so focused on the ABSOLUTE NECESSITY of co-parenting that my right to live an abuse-free life was completely taken away from me. He was the father of my child, and I had to deal with him. So if he was going to act that way, I just had to figure out a way to work around it. Having a Judge actually state in court that co-parenting obviously wasn't going to work put a lot of freedom back in my corner. Suddenly, if I communicated only by email, I wasn't being difficult, I was enforcing boundaries. If I wasn't willing to accommodate his party schedule, I wasn't "interfering in his parenting time," but instead I was maintaining a stable environment. I don't know what it was that made that particular Judge realize that the behavior wasn't going to change, but I wish he'd stuck around to finish my case.

2. Absolute parallel parenting. It doesn't matter how much you compromise with a narcissist in the best interests of the kids, they will continue to gaslight and manipulate. Stick to the decree and do not deviate. Make sure that if there is parental alienation attempts like in my case, don't try to defend or bad

mouth the other parent. Keep the child out of the middle. Even though it hurts, your children will see the "grownup." Don't be too passive either. Correct lies but then focus on your relationship with your child and with an abundance of love. We do everything with minimal contact and even then, it's nearly impossible to come to co-parenting decisions. They want control and will turn any situation into a battlefield. For instance, my last contact was about registering one of my sons for baseball. A simple question of would he be able to share in the cost and the commitment to taking him to practices and games was met with a two-page scathing diatribe over my bad mothering because I moved 40 miles away and how terrible that is to "his" son. How I make "his" son suffer with a long commute and he would only agree with one condition, if I would reimburse him for any missed practices because that would be a waste of HIS resources. Never mind the fact that my husband and I have been our kids coaches for 3 out of the past seasons and took him to every single practice and game and I paid for my portion of registration and 100% of expenses. When I told him that fact and no, I would not accept his conditions, the response I received back was "oh yeah, you are so high and mighty you make me laugh, fluffing your feathers to try to be better." I gave up. I responded with "Never mind, this isn't worth it. I'm paying the entire registration and I'll forward the schedule. If you want to participate, great. If not, great." Another abusive email was received and ignored and the next day I received a text "So, I'll pay my portion and take him to practice on my days." They just can't do that initially!

3. Just always keep in mind to respond only about the matters regarding kids. If they become confrontational, don't engage or defend. Use only email contact so you have a paper trail. My ex narcissist likes to throw out things from a year or two ago, and I simply forward the past conversation to correct his skewed perception. Even something in writing, they will deny. Make sure your conversations are only about medical information, sharing important school information or other custodial issues. The less contact, the less abuse you will need

to endure. And it only takes one to disengage. If the narcissist tries to accuse you of something that is false, respond by saying, "Your attempt to portray me in a negative light is noted."

4. I've had a major "three strikes you're out" co-parenting experience. Since I've been burned, I just do my best to parallel parent. If you ever remind them about coats, lunches, medicine, you are trying to tell them how to be a good dad and they ALWAYS take it as a narcissistic insult; AKA my "weekly bitch remark" about his parenting. Even coordinating Christmas this year, I sent him a list of gifts I was getting off of the kids' list so we wouldn't have duplicates. He had parenting time Christmas morning (I had Christmas afternoon) so he made sure he got exactly what I bought them and doubled it. Also, when the kids and I donated to the Children's Museum to teach them what it means to give and be grateful to "one up" me, he took our 2yr and 4yr old to a homeless camp under a bridge and started handing out hundreds of dollars. Always trying to outdo me. I keep to myself and just do my best to reverse the damage when they come home.

5. I would only agree to co-parent by email only as its authenticity is easier to prove with forensic science than text messages. Since text by PC was introduced it has not been successfully traced back to the originating source because some IP addresses are masked. E-mail through a Google account can be traced and authenticated. My ex-narcissist has spliced recordings, introducing them as evidence and I had to fight to get them thrown out due to lack of chain of custody, failure to produce authentication, etc. I have been advised by a forensic technological expert that email is the best route. I can document everything. Co-parenting with a narcissist is especially difficult. Keeping a no contact rule, and emailing only about parenting custodial issues, is the only way to go. I am petitioning for sole legal because my ex-narcissist has literally used our joint custody arrangement to prevent treatment of our child and he uses that arrangement to gain

access to me. Domestic violence by proxy even in its mildest form is a tactic used with medical practitioners, law enforcement, our children, court systems, therapists, and GALs. It's the narcissist's way of continuing to deliver terror, keeping chaos and turmoil going, and deflecting from the real issues. It is just another smear campaign tactic, especially for those who suffer from PTSD or any sort of battered spouse syndrome.

6. At first, when we separated and got divorced it was not parallel parenting. It was me doing sole parenting as I had done in the marriage. I truly believe that parallel parenting only comes about when the narcissist has an audience. If left to his own devices he'd leave the daily drudgery of parenting to someone else. In my case parallel parenting came because of the new girlfriend who turned into a live-in and then the step-mom. I felt that once he "hooked" her he had to show her that he was the wonderful father he claimed to be. That's when the custody suits started. During the custody battle, I believe the step-mother was the one who crossed more boundaries and did more damage to my kids than he did. I think she decided, encouraged by him because of their "absent (can we say projection) mother" to be their "new, more wonderful mother" and proceeded to take them to doctors, sign permission slips to drop classes, discuss problems with teachers, etc., while introducing herself to people as <first name> <same last name as kids>. These were things that I solely did for years because the children simply didn't have another parent who did them. (e.g. daughter 8 had surgery. Ex didn't show up but expected me to drive son to hockey and leave daughter at home.) In one teacher's conference that she arranged and I showed up to, the step-mom tried to drive the conversation. I asked that the teacher conference be a conversation between the PARENTS only and proceeded to discuss the problem (my ex sat there like a lump because he didn't have anything to say yet told the facilitator later that I verbally abused his wife). A parent facilitator helped me greatly in establishing boundaries and, even though the narcissist insisted that the step-mother was

their mother, the facilitator kept telling him that she was not and, no, she didn't have the same rights as me, as he claimed. I have to wonder how many women out there raise their children on their own only to have the children taken over by a new woman. In my experience a narcissist doesn't parent at all. That's too hum drum and doesn't give any narcissistic supply. My ex put it best through his pure projecting statement of "She only provides for the children for show." If that statement doesn't define him I don't know what does.

Sheltering the Children

One of the most difficult parts of this battle is the fight to protect your children during a high conflict divorce. In normal divorces, it is inevitable that one or both parents will do or say something along the way that they will regret. The key factors here are that the offending parent recognizes their actions as harmful and will have remorse for said offense. While two normal parents may disagree about finances or other nuances, they are generally able to put their differences aside when it comes to protecting their children from the rollercoaster ride of divorce.

It defies logic to think that a parent would actually hurt a child for their own gain and then have zero remorse for doing so. It is unfathomable to think that such actions are not isolated incidences but calculated decisions that are planned out, ongoing and will obviously have long-term effects on the children. It is incredibly difficult to explain the actions of a narcissist to a logical, healthy person because, as we've established, the narcissist's actions defy logic. The rational mind cannot conceive that someone would purposefully hurt a child and therefore, it reasons, the healthy parent must be paranoid, bitter and full of exaggerations. There is nothing further from the truth. A narcissist only cares about himself and winning. Therefore, he would hurt a child if there was something for him to gain.

At the beginning of our divorce, I discovered that Seth was setting up a video camera and trying to escalate the girls' emotions during our custody exchanges. I found it odd that he would say good-bye and then continue to come back into their bedroom to tell them how sad he would be without them or how much he was going to miss them. On one such encounter, he went into their bedroom three separate times until they were hysterical. As I was in their bedroom trying to calm them, I noticed a video camera on the floor. I couldn't believe that Seth would do this to them in an effort to obtain a video tape of them crying for the courts.

I wrote Seth an email that night begging him to stop. On that email, I cc'd my Aunt Bev, who has been my rock, role model and mother-figure for my entire life. Because she works in the mental health profession, she was able to see to the core of the issue: Narcissistic Personality Disorder. This was her response to my email:

> *Tina- This is about as cold and manipulative as you can get. How could Seth do this to those sweet, innocent little girls? Once again, selfish doesn't even begin to explain this. Seth is about as narcissistic as they come. What is so sad to me is that he has to stage situations to try to show he is a good father. How about actually being a good father? That kind of behavior is not being a good father.....over and over again this stuff happens. This kind of thinking becomes a safety issue as it only takes one selfish thought, one selfish moment for a horrible accident to occur when children are under the care of an adult. It is sad to have to wish that the girls grow up quickly so they can be safe with him.*
>
> *He keeps wanting you to forgive him for being such a selfish, manipulative partner and father--and yet he keeps doing this stuff over and over and over. He doesn't get it. All of his behavior is justifiable in his mind. He is a textbook case of Narcissist Personality Disorder. Several years ago when you first started filling me in on what was happening in your marriage, I didn't know that I would see the actual development of a narcissist. I have only seen a narcissist at this current stage--fully developed. Clinically this would have been interesting to watch if it hadn't been my family suffering through it all. This hasn't been interesting....it's been a nightmare. I give you a lot of credit for staying so well-grounded through all of the insanity.*
>
> *What really concerns me is that now that you are not having some daily, positive influence on Seth, how his narcissism is going to progress--especially in light of the fact that his mother is now influencing him so much. Cleo is truly the most ill, destructive*

person I have ever witnessed. That says a lot. I've seen a lot of very, very ill people in my job....but I have never seen anyone so ill and destructive as that woman. She has nurtured such sickness in her children. Cleo is a "wolf in sheep's clothing." I know that Leonard is very ill but Cleo wins the prize in this family. Her influence is what started Seth's path to illness and now that she is his primary influence again I shudder to think where this will take him--and who he will take down with him. The mother bear has come out in me too. Although the social worker in me still keeps my compassion for Seth alive....it is getting harder and harder to keep that in the mix when I see him hurting you and the girls over and over and over. I have no compassion for Cleo. I believe she is smart and knows better.

When I think of him PLANNING to make the girls cry--him setting up the camera and making sure that it was in the right spot! As a parent you do everything in your power to keep your kids from hurting--you don't hurt them on purpose.....you especially don't PLAN to do it. I am thankful you are there for the girls. I'm glad that you are mentally healthy. With you in their life they have a chance to break Seth's cycle of destruction. I love you with all my heart. Be safe. -Auntie

At that point in time, and even with the guidance of my Aunt, I still didn't understand that Seth's behaviors were truly a result of Narcissistic Personality Disorder. It was spelled out in front of me (literally) but I was so overwhelmed that I couldn't even think straight. All I knew was that I had to protect my children with every ounce of my being. I read by Aunt's email, but I was in a daze and didn't absorb the part about NPD. I knew he was sick and that was the extent of my understanding at that time.

Almost six months later, I retained possession of the video camera and became physically ill while watching the videos that Seth had made of our children. He videotaped their reaction after he gutted the house of our possessions and he videotaped them in the bathtub as he discussed changing their preschool. He was asking our daughter for her opinion on switching to the preschool that he wanted her to attend with no consideration for the fact that she was only four years old or that this was the preschool she had attended for 1.5 years. There was no reason for her to switch preschools except that Seth knew it would upset me. This was the preschool that I signed Piper up for when I was pregnant with her because the waiting list was over two years long. Seth's video tapes contained audio which showcased his manic, creepy voice and unstable mental condition. To this day, five years later, I cannot watch those tapes.

This type of behavior continued for years. Seth told the girls that my name was "T-Rex" despite their tears. He taped my photo over with blue electrical tape and mounted it on their fireplace regardless of how it affected the girls. Seth growled at them and acted like a bear until my youngest daughter was hysterical and he continuously scared them by saying that they would have to start staying at his house overnight. He had no regard for their feelings when we first separated and, five years later, he still doesn't care how his actions affect them. Seth defines what it is like to divorce someone with Narcissistic Personality Disorder and as obvious as it was to me, I struggle to understand why the courts did not see the writing on the wall.

Answers from the Battlefield:

1. You don't talk or discuss about adult matters around the children. If the ex is acting mean, or using a bad tone of voice, I always kept calm, spoke nicely, or didn't say anything in return, because I wanted the atmosphere as calm as possible when my son was present. I never wanted to throw more gas on the fire. I knew I was fighting a losing battle to try and discuss anything with the ex narcissist, or share my comment, so, to stay out of the battle, I knew to keep my mouth shut during exchanges. If our son comes home and shares with me something Daddy said about Mommy, I nip it in the bud, and say, "I don't know why Daddy would say that." Then, I would document and put it behind me!! If Daddy couldn't attend an event for our son, and our son was unhappy, I would tell our son, "We are going to have fun and be happy whether Daddy is here or not." It's not calling and complaining and griping to the ex narcissist. This gets me nowhere. Instead, it's giving lots of love, communication, and making ground rules that nothing is allowed to take the happiness out of my home. We have to be the peacemaker with a bear. If two bears get into a

disagreement, then a major fight or death could occur. I know peace is the answer with this type of person, and this is how I shelter my son.

2. Read all you can to arm yourself with knowledge about narcissism and boundaries. Implement what you learn and stop being a narcissistic supply to ex. Get therapy for kids and yourself. Focus on teaching children emotional awareness and empathy along with boundary setting. Never criticize their father as a person, but help them to recognize inappropriate behavioral choices. Understand yourself that the emotional abuse of narcissist is domestic violence. Use the support services of a local DV agency, which often have support groups for you and children and can recommend skilled lawyers and therapists who "get it." Develop a strong social support group for yourself including "One Mom's Battle." Make your children's daily lives, or the time you are with them if you are noncustodial parent safe, loving times. Keep a firm goal of protecting your children in whatever situation you are in. For us that meant slugging through the court system for sole legal and physical custody and supervised visitation. It took years, the contribution of family members for legal fees, a bull dog attorney, a talented GAL, selling personal items for legal fees, tenacity, and the stupid behaviors of narcissist and family, but our goal was achieved and the children now have peace.

3. I advise having clear boundaries with drop-offs and pick-ups – he is not allowed in the home – he either waits in his car or on the porch --- do not let him in the house, because it gives him power. I learned the hard way. My ex-husband used to secretly audio tape his visits including the drop-offs and pick-ups and would purposely start a fight with the kids. He would ask the same question over and over about things that we had already discussed to push our buttons. He was clearly trying show that I was a bad mom, and trying to say I was turning the kids against them and that the kids were afraid of me. While we got upset, he would be calm and cool and then he would then say things like, "Why are you sticking your finger in my face?" or "Why

did you grab me like that? Look at how angry you get!" He would say that I looked crazed when in fact that was not the case – none of those actions ever occurred. At one point, his attorney sent an audio recording to my attorney and at first she was furious with me. When she let me hear it, I told her to not listen to how we were all crying but to what we were saying and the content of what was being said. He purposefully would push his way into my house and get in my face intimidating me --- once she and our psychologist re-listened to the tape and had the conversation written out – our words on paper – it became apparent what he was doing. Several times, you could hear me or the kids say, "No one is even near you. Who is putting a finger in your face? No one touched you." ... I learned the hard way --- he would stop at nothing to win.

4. Always do the right thing. You can hang your hat on that. If you always live with honor and integrity, in the end your child will have been exposed to the appropriate way to act/live. I feel they never forget that "base." They may detour, etc. but I honestly believe they will return to what they have learned is "the right way" to live. Answer questions as honestly as possible – keeping in mind the age of the child and the nature of the question. Never belittle your ex. I think using bad decisions as a learning opportunity for kids (depending on the situation) is a good idea, though. I try to be as honest and straightforward as I can possibly be in the hopes that my daughter will feel she can trust me enough to talk to me about anything – without fear. I know she knows my love is unconditional. I also am very aware that she feels her father's love comes with strings. She may not be able to put that into words just yet, but she knows mom will be there – no matter what. That has to be enough for now. The rest is up to time and experience. I pray every day that my child grows up to be a normal, happy individual who demonstrates a healthy balance of empathy, independence, self-confidence and integrity.

5. Be the strong, reasonable, safe parent. Even though you feel broken and the narcissist is spewing lies about you, hold your

head up high and continue to be a good person. Make your home a place of peace and safety, a refuge from the storm. Only talk about the narcissist "as needed," and when he does crazy things, let the kids know that they're safe by remaining strong, consistent, and level-headed yourself. Kids naturally gravitate to a place of peace and safety. I try to create a "narcissist free" home...if they must talk to me about his behavior, that's okay, but otherwise he doesn't even exist in our home or our day-to-day life. Let the children know that they are your number one priority. Laughter is wonderful. Even children as young as 5 can see how far-fetched and ridiculous the narcissist's behaviors are, and it's healing to just laugh it off with a "who knows what he's thinking!" comment. Don't ever involve them in adult issues such as money, etc. When the kids bring these things up, I tell them those are adult issues and not to worry about them. I let them know again and again that I'm the grownup, and everything will be okay. I let them know I can handle anything he throws at us, and that their only job is to be children...to play and go to school. All 5 of the children prefer to be with me, in a house with safety, peace, routine, support, love, and consistency. The narcissist inevitably hangs himself with his crazy, criminal behavior...at. My attorney always said "just give him the rope and watch him hang himself." Just breathe, keep things routine, and let them be kids. In the beginning you will have to pretend to be strong, and eventually you WILL be strong. You will have to force yourself to do the day-to-day routine things for them. Just do it. They need at least one strong, stable, consistent parent more than anything. Narcissists are incapable of this. You're all they have.

Breaking the Cycle

One of Seth's greatest fears was that he would turn out like his father, Leonard. It was also my greatest fear. Their family defined dysfunction, but a terrifying way. Leonard is one of the most narcissistic individuals that I have ever met with a grandiose self-image and an incredibly elitist attitude. He had affairs throughout his entire marriage and his wife, Cleo, turned the other cheek. Seth and his oldest brother, Robert are chips off the old block in every way and, in some ways, they are even worse. During the positive times in our marriage, when things were smooth, Seth would write his father long letters detailing and addressing his disturbing behaviors but when our marriage fell apart, they formed an alliance to take me down at all costs.

Out of the entire family, my greatest anger rests with Seth's mom, Cleo. Cleo was the one who fed the narcissism in her family. She was also smart enough to know what she was doing and could have broken the cycle by getting help for her children. Cleo was the one person who could have stepped in and saved my daughters, her only granddaughters, Piper and Sarah. Yet she chose (again) to turn the other cheek. She told huge lies in court, through declarations and during both of our custody evaluations. To her, winning and protecting her family image were more important than her own granddaughters.

In 2013, Piper (age 7) was downstairs at Seth's house helping him to remove Christmas tree ornaments from the tree. Seth did not like how Piper was removing the ornaments and he grabbed her wrist roughly and, in true Seth-fashion, he squeezed her arm very hard. Piper ended up locking herself in a bathroom to get away from him and was then blocked from her phone and from going upstairs to tell Cleo. After Piper was allowed upstairs, she tried to lock herself in a bathroom and Seth forced his way in. Piper found Cleo and explained what happened while crying. Cleo's response to 8-year old Piper, "Let's try to figure out a way that your dad can handle his anger better."

Really? How about calling the police and reporting that your son just assaulted your granddaughter? To make matters worse, Seth (with Cleo present) made Piper sit down and write down all of the positive things that had happened that day. Initially, Piper refused and then Seth promised her a dance party if she honored his request. She hesitated but finally relented. They never had a dance party. Piper, Sarah and I spent that evening at our local police station filing a report for assault against a child. Weeks later, Child Welfare services closed the case and the DA decided not to press charges.

This is a quote from Cleo taken from an email to Seth at the beginning stages of our divorce, *"Think of this as a chess game; you have to outsmart her and if you react emotionally, you'll be feeding right into her game plan, NOT yours."*

My goal from the time I began to understand NPD was to break the sick cycle created and perpetuated by Seth's family. Unknowingly, I had been grooming my oldest daughter by following parenting advice handed down from Cleo and Leonard. I was to praise my daughter for how smart she was and constantly boast about her talents to friends, family and strangers. This was more than the behavior of a proud mom, these were the actions of a family determined to create another entitled, egotistical person to carry on the family name. While every parent wants their child to feel special and praised, this was extreme grooming and I had become an unknowing participant.

Since my marriage ended in 2009, I have been on a mission to reverse the damage that had been done to my children. While Seth had visitation it was difficult, because I knew what they were hearing at Seth's family's home. Common topics range from how fat certain family members had become, to homophobic and racial slurs. Over the years, our daughters would have surely memorized their grandparents' and father's SAT scores and heard about how their mother didn't have a college degree. I have used every available opportunity to reverse what they had learned and I am proud to say that I have been successful as a mom. I have two incredible little girls who are extremely caring and empathic.

In today's world, I believe that it is important to teach empathy regardless of if the child has a narcissistic parent or not. I have coined my approach "Empathy Boot Camp," and here are just a few of the things that I have done to ensure that I am raising healthy, happy and kind members of our society:

- Use everyday things such as Lost Dog posters to show empathy. I will often point out posters and ask, "How do you think that family feels? Sad, scared, etc?"

- We carry small paper bags (from our church) filled with items such as bottled water, granola bar, new socks, toothbrush and other needed items in our car and deliver them to homeless people that we encounter while we are out and about.

- For $35 per month, we've adopted a little girl from Africa. Our little "Limpho" has become a part of my daughters' lives and is often the topic of conversations. Her picture is posted on our kitchen bulletin board as a daily reminder of how fortunate we are.

- On Thanksgiving or other holidays, we have driven around town with plates of food to deliver to those less fortunate and at Christmas-time, we look forward to delivering platters of cookies to those at our local homeless day camp.

My step-son recently lost his friend in a horrific car accident and I saw the results of our empathy work first-hand. After a 24-hour stay in the hospital, we received the news that his friend had been removed from life support. My daughters had never even met this young man but both began to cry because their step-brother was hurting. Hours later, Piper emerged from her room with a hand-made card for her brother. The card read, *"I am so sorry your friend died. I could never even image what you are going through. Just remember that Kyle is in a good place where God can be with him and he is in no pain. That might make you feel a bit better."*- Piper

The cycle is broken. My daughters are as beautiful on the inside as they are on the outside. They know that being kind is more important than being right. They know they are loved for who they are and not for how smart they are or what they accomplish. They know how to take ownership for their actions. I model that by admitting to and apologizing for anything that I've done wrong. They know that everyone's voice is important. We discuss boundaries and how to handle a situation when someone crosses those boundaries.

Answers from the Battlefield:

1. We talk about feelings and how we are held accountable for our mistakes. It's important to have a counselor. Also, we pray together and are working on being healthy, and not sweeping things under the rug. I'm a domestic violence advocate and survivor, so this has been my approach to getting healthy.

2. My biggest fear is that my daughters will choose husbands like their father. I can already see some of the same passive behaviors in them that I had with their dad. My oldest daughter avoids all conflict, is very passive, internalizes her emotions, is fearful and very compliant in her relationships. My youngest daughter is much more assertive in her relationships except with her father. She compliments him all the time, never

disagrees with him and worries constantly about his approval. She does not share with him that she wants to become a Mormon (she is waiting until she is 18), go to BYU and marry a Mormon. Her father is an atheist and wants her to go to his alma mater.

To break the cycle of the bad example I have set, I:

- Attempt every day to be a better example.

- Expose them to non-violent relationships.

- Take them to therapy.

- We are all taking a PSI workshop in a few months.

- Write them a note every day about strength, confidence, peacefulness and gratitude. And tell them something positive about them that has nothing to do with their looks or having a boyfriend.

- Sending my youngest to an all-girls Catholic High School (yes, the one who wants to be a Mormon) so that she does not feel the pressure of having to become less than she is and acquiesce to boys, fashion, peer pressure about sex, alcohol, etc.

3. I'm glad to know I'm not the only one feeling this! I have been feeling guilty for thinking about this because I have seen some concerning traits. I am always sure to stay consistent with discipline and talk to my son about consequences-good or bad. I also try to teach empathy and how to put yourself in other people's shoes.

4. Recently my daughter has started saying mean things followed up by "I'm just joking." A habit she's learned from her father. I've spent time explaining to her that saying "I'm joking" is not an excuse to hurt people's feelings. Every day is damage control when you co-parent with a narcissist.

5. Teaching empathy, compassion, and telling the truth. The

comment above regarding the "I'm joking" excuse scares me. That's what my exN said to me repeatedly after saying hurtful things. I didn't know what gaslighting was back then.

"Live so that when your children think of fairness, caring, and integrity, they think of you." -H. Jackson Brown, Jr.

LIFE BEYOND N.P.D.

Contrary to what the narcissist in your life has led you to believe, there is life after the narcissist. I am living proof that there can be a peaceful existence on the other side. No matter how young your children are, you have the ability to set boundaries and take your power back in all aspects of your life. You have the choice to remain a victim or to become a survivor.

Part of the journey to regain control of your life is a mindset that starts with proclaiming your new beginning. Say the words out loud: "I am a survivor," and write them on your mirror to serve as a daily affirmation until the thought moves from the hope stage to that of a solid mindset. Of course, you will have setbacks along the way and down days. The key is to allow yourself to have these days with zero guilt and then dust yourself off and climb right back into the saddle. If you didn't have down days, you wouldn't be human.

Finding (Real) Love

As the child of very young, divorced parents I carried several loads of heavy baggage into adulthood. I craved stability and a marriage that was forever. I made the same mistake that so many make: I was looking for love and happiness in all the wrong places. I was looking for love outside of my own heart.

When I was in love, I could distract myself from my childhood issues and pains. After a series of failed relationships, I stopped dating for a year to work on myself. I needed to learn to love myself, which was something that I had never been taught. Despite how confident I felt by the end of my year-long dating hiatus, I was no match for the snake-like charm of a narcissist. I believed that people were who they said they were and felt how they claimed to. I had never heard of Narcissistic Personality Disorder and didn't realize that I was about to be swept off my feet by a Prince who turned into a frog shortly after our courtship began.

People often ask me how I had the ability to ever love or trust again. You'd have to know me to understand. I am a trusting person and I see the best in people. I love life and I am both positive and happy by nature. By becoming bitter, jaded and sad, I'd let Seth win. I had let his shadow affect the quality of my life for way too long. I left because I wanted to bask in the sunshine far away from the reach of his shadows.

When I met my husband, Richard, I had no intention of dating anyone. I had recently made a list of the 50 things that I wanted in a partner and in my mind; it was a list that I would be pulling out and referencing over and over for a very long time. At that point in time, I was separated from Seth but we had not even filed for divorce so a relationship was not even a fleeting thought in my head. During a search to find new friends outside of my "married friend group," I had coffee with Richard and that encounter turned into a second coffee date hours later and the rest is history. We were married in April of 2013 after dating for almost four years and it was the best decision that I've ever made.

Richard has been my rock and my shelter throughout this hurricane. He has learned about narcissism as I've learned about it. Ironically, he was impressed when we first met because of the mature nesting agreement that Seth and I had. Little did he or I know what was in store when Seth began going off the deep end. Thankfully, he has stood by my side through it all.

Richard and I started our relationship very slowly. We didn't rush things. Our relationship started as a friendship and remains a friendship five years later. I am proud of the relationship that I have and I cherish the man that I am married to. I am thankful that I didn't meet Richard 15 years ago because as a 25-year-old girl, I would have never appreciated the man that I share my life with now. For the first time ever, I can actually visualize myself growing old with someone.

I believe that God knew I couldn't handle another bad relationship. He answered my prayers and placed a man in my life that mirrored my list of 50 qualifications that I wanted in a future partner. I had made a promise to myself that I wouldn't settle when it came to any area of my life. I loved myself and my daughters too much to continue settling. I believe that in order to find a healthy relationship, you must love and respect yourself completely. You must pay attention to red flags and you must use borrowed judgment. Dr. Craig Malkin, clinical psychologist and instructor in psychology at Harvard Medical School shares the following tips:

> *"Pay attention to feedback from friends, for instance. They're more apt to see -- and remember -- important red flags that you miss, precisely because they're not under the spell (I call this 'borrowed judgment'). Keep a journal of painful moments, and ask yourself, is your partner working with you to understand and prevent them? Learn, and watch out for, some of the hallmarks of narcissism: Is every mistake he makes, for example, someone else fault ('externalizing')? Does she routinely devalue and belittle other people in her stories? If so, it's only a matter of time before the disdain or indifference comes your way."*

Don't be afraid to love again. There are a lot of very good people in this world and while we all know there are bad seeds, don't allow them to continue to rule your life. There is no timeframe that is right. It is right when you feel ready. No one can decide what is right for you – it could be two months or it could be five years. One of my favorite poems is "You Learn" by Jorge Luis Borges which was taped to my refrigerator for a very long time as a daily reminder:

You Learn

After a while you learn the subtle difference

Between holding a hand and chaining a soul,

And you learn that love doesn't mean leaning

And company doesn't mean security.

And you begin to learn that kisses aren't contracts

And presents aren't promises,

And you begin to accept your defeats

With your head up and your eyes open

With the grace of a woman, not the grief of a child,

And you learn to build all your roads on today

Because tomorrow's ground is too uncertain for plans

And futures have a way of falling down in mid-flight.

After a while you learn...

That even sunshine burns if you get too much.

So you plant your garden and decorate your own soul,

Instead of waiting for someone to bring you flowers.

And you learn that you really can endure...

That you really are strong

And you really do have worth...

And you learn and learn...

With every good-bye you learn.

Advice from the Battlefield:

1. Prior to dating, make a pact with someone you can trust to have discernment. Promise to them & yourself to take their advice, then be intentional in letting that person discern with you the people you date. This person needs to be a human Narc Decoder. Like Tina said, it's common to disregard the warning signs given to us by our closest friends & family.

2. Look at who has been there for you, who has seen you at your worst and your best, and who truly believes in you. Look at the way they treat you on a daily basis, not in "romantic" moments.... how they treat you when talking about money, or

household tasks, or putting together IKEA furniture. Look at how they interact with your child(ren). Those are the real tests. Learning to recognize old habits and patterns is really important.

3. Love yourself first. I cannot emphasize this enough. Buy yourself flowers, take yourself to a fancy restaurant and leave your comfort zone. Love isn't supposed to hurt. Ever. Before you try to perfect love with someone else, perfect it within your own heart first.

4. It will be two years tomorrow that I fled a domestic violence situation. I've done a lot of work personally, spiritually and on myself in general. I've been raising my daughter with the help of my loving family here in beautiful Florida, finishing up a degree I never thought would happen. I'm dating a man friends introduced me to, and he's nothing short of amazing. He knows my story, and is so loving and supportive. I took my time. I listened to what I wanted and my boundaries. I stick to them!!!

5. I'm not even close to dating yet, but I have seen a pattern from reading everyone else's stories. It seems that deciding someone is "fantastic" too quickly is a common trap. By too quickly, I mean what might be a normal pace for people who haven't been involved in a toxic relationship. From what I've read, I think it would take at least a year or two of really getting to know someone, and giving them plenty of opportunities to make mistakes and handle stressful situations before I would move into a "serious" relationship or introduce anyone to my children. Maybe not many men will want to stick around for that slow a pace, but I can live with that.

The New Feed Supply

When Seth and I first began dating, he fed me tales of how close he was with all of his ex-girlfriends. I had always heard that this was a good sign, so it was a huge plus to me. He told me that he still sent them birthday cards and checked in with them every once in a while. He pressed me on whether or not this would bother me if our relationship progressed and I wasn't sure how to answer the question. I let him know that as long as it was completely platonic and that the communication remained open and not hidden, I didn't think that I would have a problem with it.

Months turned into years. I never heard another word about this topic, which seemed strange to me. A conversation with Seth's older brother, Robert, left me convinced that my initial conversation with Seth was filled with lies. According to Robert, Seth didn't date in high school nor did he date in college. For many years, Robert said he actually thought that Seth was gay. Seth's awkwardness in the bedroom further proved to me that he had never really dated or had sexual experience in any way, shape or fashion. In the ten years that I knew him, there was never another mention of an ex-girlfriend.

I knew how socially awkward Seth was in social settings and imagined that his post-divorce dating life would be a complete train wreck fueled by alcohol. I had heard of multiple short-lived romances that he managed after our split but there had never been anyone who I would refer to as a girlfriend until 2012. As I walked into our neighborhood Kinkos to photocopy some court documents, I saw them out of the corner of my eye. Seth entered Kinkos right behind me followed by a blonde girl who was dutifully carrying his huge stack of court paperwork. He and I made eye contact and he looked away nervously but never told her that his evil ex-wife, the one who was preventing a loving father from visiting his children, was standing five feet away. Minnie was small, meek and attractive. She looked like she could be my younger sister.

Shortly after that encounter, we discovered that there was Minnie on the West Coast and Sharon on the East Coast. The distance between them was a narcissist's dream. I was baffled when I found out that Seth had told my daughters that he was going to get married soon to Sharon, Minnie or another pretty girl. Who says that? Apparently, Seth does. Shortly after that, I was notified by a mutual friend of some photos on Seth's Facebook page which appeared to be engagement photos. Through a bit of internet exploration, we actually found the photos and low and behold, they were engagement photos.

I've never met Seth's fiancé, Sharon, because their engagement only lasted a short time (shocking, I know), but I did meet Minnie at visitation exchanges. We never said a word to each other, but the girls spoke very highly of her and I had to remind myself that the girls were safer when she was around. As expected, she did choose to mettle in our custody battle on multiple occasions. The first time was when Seth called the girls extremely intoxicated on Father's Day and I notified Minor's Counsel. Minnie went to bat for Seth and stated that she was with him and he was sober. During our final custody evaluation, Minnie defended Seth to the evaluator as a stellar father who loved his children more than life itself. She shared examples of how wonderful he was with the children when she was around. Key words here are: *when she was around.*

Through our divorce proceedings, I was contacted by a total of three women who had dated Seth. Two offered to appear in person to testify on my behalf and all three wrote declarations about their experiences with him. I hear a lot of horror stories from the battlefield and I am thankful that Seth never aligned with a person who was equally as evil as he is. I am thankful that Minnie was able to be along for some of Seth's visits which, ultimately, made them easier to handle because I knew the girls were safe.

Advice from the Battlefield:

1. The step-mother is the problem in our situation. Not only is she a narcissist herself but she lives in another world – she is not centered in reality. I had to learn that her reality is not what is truly happening. I have told my son that it is okay for him to love her, but I don't have to share those feelings. I also had to accept that she has no desire to get along with me and she thrives on drama. That she views me as a threat to her relationship and therefore, she keeps the pot stirred. Now I only communicate when the father wants information. I don't have to be the glue in his relationship with my son, and as long as she is in the picture there is very little hope for a healthy relationship.

2. It's difficult. I know that he spun the new girlfriend (GF) a whole heap of lies and she started working with him and, sometimes even harder than him, to fight the 'nasty ex-wife' (me) who wouldn't let him see his kids. All of it was untrue, of course. She wrote affidavits for his court case – and there was one I had to laugh at. My ex cheated our whole marriage and fathered twin daughters while married to me. He admitted

to that in an email to a third party and I put that in my court papers (I needed orders that he not be able to expose the children to porn, etc.) The email also tells how he hid his infidelity with secret mobile phones, etc. Her affidavit said that he had no problem with sex and that they were in a monogamous relationship! I had to laugh because I knew he was still up to his online sex hunt (credit card bills I still got). She also turned up at my house once to pick up the kids (too long a story to explain here) when I wasn't sending them and I had to call the police to move her on. Her affidavit about that incident was full of lies. She is as narcissistic as him. When she moved in with him the lies and manipulation on his part increased. I know she wrote some of his emails. He calls the children far more often when she is with him and pretty much ignores them when she is away from him – so yes, he acts the loving dad in front of her. Many tales to tell about this situation. So yes, definitely, the harassment escalated when she came on the scene.

3. Until my ex-narcissist's new wife entered the picture, he was an absentee father. Even when we were still married. He always said he never wanted our son to begin with. He would routinely "forget" it was his parenting time and would not show up or call. When he did take my son, their time together consisted of "ordering pizza and watching TV." Then she entered the picture and suddenly he wanted to be father of the year. All of a sudden the long, in-depth, detailed trips and experiences started. Suddenly there was no more take out and it all "gourmet" meals. Then, after they were married, the fighting for more time and custody began. Now the Ex-narcissist's narcissistic wife thinks she is my son's mother! She routinely tries to get in my face and yell at me. She actively tries to bully me as much as the ExN. She tries to tell me how to raise my child. This is a woman who has never had kids and has no legal right to my son. Normally I ignore her and don't allow her to ruffle my feathers. I have had to threaten to call the police when she has gotten in my face. I don't allow her to see me upset or annoyed. The most recent

time was at a Boy Scout event where I had to threaten to call the police in front of the entire Boy Scout pack and parents. When she hears authorities are going to be called she backs off. She has bad-mouthed me to my son several times. My son is very defensive of me and has told her to back off and not to talk about his mom. (I know my ex hates that).

No matter how heated or upset I am, my current husband would never get in my ex's face or tell him what to do with my son on his time. No matter how much my husband hates my ex, he won't ever cross the line or show disrespect to him as a parent in front of my son. He knows to have the police on speed dial and ready to call, but won't put us in a bad situation. And I appreciate that. My husband always supports me, but he knows how to protect and support without giving the ExN what he wants (a fight). As a divorced parent I don't see how allowing your new spouse to abuse your ex is helpful to anyone! The best advice I can give is just stay strong. Remember, the more they see us as mothers upset, the more they will attack. If they know something bothers you, they will use it against you at every turn. They will use your pain against you. So don't let them know it hurts. Don't let them know things bother you. And keep contact as minimal as possible. Most importantly, remember you are Mom. Your kids know that and know you are the safe place and that you truly love them.

4. I was the Step-Mom. I believed everything he told me about why he was comfortable with only seeing them one week in the summer and the week of Christmas. I had my own child of the same age group and I believed him when he told me he was allowed this visitation or nothing. Every raise in pay I got (he didn't get pay raises) was sent as a voluntary raise in child support. Every 'painful revelation' he convinced me of regarding what they were being raised to believe, I was expected to address with my step-kids. Every dictate of expected behavior in HIS house, I had to enforce.

When they turned 18 and moved off to college it was my insistence and the kids' efforts that kept a relationship going between him and them. I credit their Mom and Step-Dad with raising such compassionate people. My own child was unwittingly raised to be the victim of another narcissist. I really didn't know his motives behind every tension and difficult confrontation while they were growing up. I do see now that all of the odd directives were delivered by me. They had no way of knowing I was following orders. How could they? I didn't know either. He manipulated us all with a steady stream of tears and sobbing any time his directives were questioned. All of us would do anything to make him stop crying. Fast forward 23 years. His two are happily married, well-adjusted adults. There are two grandchildren too. When he left me, he also left the only child he ever raised. My child.

He now concentrates on visiting his out-of-state kids on a regular basis and teaching my grandchildren to call me by my first name instead of Grandma. It's a little secret their parents aren't aware of yet. I'm not financially able to visit them. My child is deeply entrenched with a narcissist who has severely impacted any family contact with me or the siblings. I am the Step-Mom. I really thought I was fighting for the kids at the time. And I'm truly sorry.

5. My point of view is also from the step-mom perspective. I was given the active step-mom role right off the top. I was engaged with my stepson, active in his school, sports, etc. I handled many of the doctor appointments, etc...and both mom and dad urged and allowed it to happen. To me, it was the perfect step-family dynamic. I did a lot of the communication with mom because we all thought my lines of communication were more open than Dad's and I could handle the situations more effectively. Things were great like this for quite a few years, or so I thought. Once we all moved away from each other the dynamic changed and when N and I started having problems it changed more. Mom and I were friends. I did talk

to her about certain issues he and I were having, to make sure I wasn't completely off-base with my feelings. When we separated (the first time) we both helped each other in our custody stuff. She told me that N became a better father when I came into the picture. She was aware it was because I was making him be more engaged with our son and, since I was more active with him, he had no choice but to do the same. She was the first person to point out to me he was an N. I had never heard the term before then. Then when N convinced me to go back, she kept telling me how she fell for his tricks, too, not to fall for it, etc. And when I did, she turned her back on me instantly because N told her I had shared things with him about her (which I never had). We didn't speak for 6 months and I tried to make amends for child's sake, but she ignored it. The harassment and abuse started from that end, too. To the point where it became too much to bear. N wasn't standing up for me where she was concerned. She was causing issues in my relationship with my step-son, etc., to the point where I had to disengage from that entire dynamic altogether. I sought help/support in step-parent groups and let them all do their own things unless it immediately affected my kids or our livelihoods in our home. When we filed for divorce, this time the Mom wrote an affidavit on N's behalf stating how much I hated step-son and a bunch of other lies. Things that N projected from himself onto me. I believe she is probably an N too, but in a different capacity. Their biggest thing is who can play the better game against the other. Because of this, I will never get involved in a step-family dynamic again if I can help it. And I would warn anyone about having a relationship of any kind with the other parent. As nice as they may seem, remember they were once fooled by the N, and it doesn't take much to fall back into that trap, even years later.

Post-Traumatic Stress Disorder

I was working on my laptop at my local Starbucks coffee shop one afternoon in July of 2013. I had just ended my custody battle and while I still felt a bit fuzzy and disoriented from the experience, I was enjoying the day and lost in my project. The door to the coffee shop opened at the same time my phone rang. Coming through the door was Seth, and calling on the phone was my husband, Richard. I had never been so happy to take a phone call.

I was physically shaking as I stayed on the phone with Richard. Seth walked in without noticing me and ordered his coffee. He walked over to the tables with his computer bag and coffee in hand to find a place to sit. My mind was in complete panic mode. The fight or flight instinct had taken over. Had I not been on the phone with Richard, I may have bolted out the back door the moment he entered Starbucks.

As he searched for an empty seat, our eyes met and I saw pure hatred and venom in his stare. He gave me "that look" – the look that lets me know that he would kill me with his bare hands if we were in a dark alley. Five seconds passed but it felt like five hours. He turned and walked out the door while I sat shaking. Not the image of "The Warrior Mom" that I portray on my blog or in my books.

Post-Traumatic Stress Disorder (PTSD) is an anxiety disorder that can bring the strongest warrior mom to her knees. It's almost as though your mind and your body disconnect and you no longer have control over your physical body. As I approach my 40th birthday, my eyesight isn't what it used to be. There was one afternoon recently when I was walking in downtown San Luis Obispo with my husband, Richard, and I stopped dead in my tracks and gasped. "There he is! Seth is right there!" My husband, being the centered and calm person that he is, looked and explained that it wasn't Seth. While I trusted him, I still found it difficult to go forward. Had I been alone I would have retreated to my car quickly. The person was not Seth and, in fact, they looked nothing like Seth.

During the beginning of my battle, I may have appeared completely "off my rocker" to anyone who didn't understand PTSD. It is one thing to have a traumatic experience and work to heal and move forward, and quite another to have the trauma continue over and over. The potential trauma is always lurking because the narcissist is a repeat offender. The abuses that he inflicts are invisible but incredibly powerful. The damage is significant and life-altering.

For the past few years, the thought of having the front door open without my husband home causes anxiety. While I was raised with guns in my home and have a healthy respect and fear of them, I never saw myself as a gun owner until I divorced a narcissist. To live every day with the thought that another individual hates you enough to kill you is life-altering.

Over time, and due to Seth's absence in my life for the past eight months, I am healing. I still jump if I am alone and see someone who resembles Seth, but I am getting better. Time does heal and the ceasefire which came in the form of a court order is helping to restore peace to my life. For that, I am thankful.

Advice from the Battlefield

1.   First, figure out that you have it sooner rather than later. I don't think many of us figure it out until we are way down the road. Next is to get a good therapist. I am currently trying something called EMDR and it actually seems to be helping me tremendously. This doesn't work on everyone but it apparently does on a lot of people with PTSD. After years of abuse amid losing custody of our kids, our brain seems to sometimes kind of fracture. Thoughts go all over the place with no way to focus. EMDR seems to connect them and to help with the pain. It's something relatively new I think. I'm no expert, but it seems to be helping me after 16 plus years of abuse from N, etc.

     I also have faith. Faith that God is in control. That He will work all this out for our good and His glory. I know He loves my girls more than I do and I know how much I love them. He wants what is best for them and for whatever reason, allowed N to keep them. I can't help them most of the time, but I ask Him to help them during those times. He is good that way!

     Journaling is good too. I couldn't for many years because I couldn't relive the day's nightmare all over again. But had I done it then, I might not be experiencing the PTSD as I am now.

     Also, find someone to talk to that "gets it." Not just someone who "understands." There is a huge difference. They don't have to have had the same experience as you, but they will have experienced some very hard things in life that allows them to "get it" when you talk.

2. Notice how you are feeling and accept it. Don't fight against it. From feeling it constantly, it now comes in really intense waves. The smallest thing can be a trigger. I was agoraphobic, now not so much. My advice is to get out more and see your friends. Making new friends now is always a huge thing for me because I get paranoid that they may somehow know the ex narc and be friends with him. That he has sent them to 'spy' on me! Or they have been party to the smear campaign against me and already believed his lies. Paranoid? Perhaps. But it's exactly the sort of thing he would do. Make friends, but use discretion. I have realized that there are some lovely, supportive people out there and not everyone is out to get you. Actually, no one is except the narcissist and his closest circle.

3. Get help as soon as you can. It took 4 years for me to be diagnosed after my ex tried to kill me because I tried to cope on my own. Now I'm in counseling. One of the things I am learning is that it is ok and normal to be scared. Accept it and stop criticizing myself for it. Realize that there will be set backs...creating a longer space between each "episode" is what I am aiming for right now. There is healing. Not complete healing, but hope, which drives everyone.

4. This may seem simple and stupid, but I use my sense of humor to cope. When I hear his voice in my head, it can rattle me. However, someone once told him they thought he sounded like Kermit the Frog when he spoke, so that's the voice I hear. Kermit telling me I'm "useless" is easier to take.

5. I think figuring out your worst triggers and finding a way, with therapy or self-reflection, to deal with it differently when it happens helps. I don't think this would work for everyone but I practiced responding differently when I was triggered. It helped when I knew it was coming and lessened what I felt

when it came from nowhere. Time helps. Also, trying to live a life while going through this (force yourself to go to lunch or movies with a friend every now and then).

Personal Growth and Healing

I saw a therapist in 2008 while I was still married to Seth. Krista was the first person to say the words, "Narcissistic Personality Disorder," and I was so angry with her. I left her office and didn't return for several years. Halfway through my divorce I sent her an email and, with my tail between my legs, I asked her to take me on as a client once again. I was in the middle of Hurricane Seth and I was drowning. While there were hundreds of available therapists in my area, I knew that Krista's office was where I needed to be.

Krista quickly told me that I was suffering from Post-Traumatic Stress Disorder (PTSD) and anxiety. It didn't help that I was living on coffee and pulling late night work sessions between my job and preparing for court. In addition, I was also a full-time single mom. I was a basket case who slept with a hammer and a can of mace under my pillow. I lived in constant fear of Seth and his declining mental state. I jumped at every sound in the middle of the night. The beeps of text messages left me nauseous and on edge.

I began seeing Krista several times per month and did a lot of reflecting – childhood, adulthood and everything in between. I pulled forth memories that I had tried to stuff down and I dealt with them. All of them. I journaled quite a bit and then I started my blog. Everything came to me so fast – the name of the blog and the direction that I would go with it. Each time I sat down to write, I felt huge weights come off my shoulders. I began a gratitude journal and there were some days that I was incredibly thankful and other days when I struggled to find something to write down. At one point, I was thankful that the grass was green. They were baby steps that grew and grew with each passing day.

I continued counseling with Krista, absorbing every recommendation that she had. At one point, Krista recommended sound therapy for my PTSD. I didn't question her. I purchased a CD that I listed to 2-3 times per day. While it felt a bit hooky to listen to strange beeps and noises, it did seem to help. I learned to set boundaries when it came to communication with Seth, and I slowly learned how to take my power back. Over time, the joy and happiness in life began to outweigh the fear and sadness.

Writing my book, "*Divorcing a Narcissist: One Mom's Battle*" was the final piece to my healing. I read everything that I could get my hands on. I was becoming empowered with education about this disorder. Each and every night I chipped away at it and, in just over six months, I found myself uploading my file to the printer and approving my book for print just 24-hours later. The moment that the UPS man rang my doorbell and handed me a package which contained my new book, hot off the press, was one of the best moments of my life. To actually hold it in my hand was the most healing thing in the world. My story. In my hands.

Advice from the Battlefield:

1. I have recently started to say that if Nelson Mandela can sit in a jail cell for 27 years, I can endure what my ex-husband does to me. It's sad to find out that when I think he can't get any worse, he manages to do something even worse. But you do find out how much you can endure, and you start to just focus on the things that matter to you. While my ex-husband actively tries to have me jailed for contempt – he continuously files bogus contempt charges – I am just happy that our child is healthy. I enjoy eating a meal with our child and having a good conversation. You find your joy where you can when things are so horrible.

2. After I learned everything I could about sociopaths and narcissists, I delved into discovering what it was about me that made me such a good target. I am no longer a good target. Education is the ultimate power.

3. I used absolutely every therapist that would see me and did a lot of soul searching. I am not done yet. Today, while I was out, I realized I come across people that I just don't like. I don't know them. They may even be silent, but my radar goes off. I think that's growth. My preservation instincts are kicking in and I have developed a warning system. I am tired of guilt, also, so I am getting ready to work on that. I have picked my broken self up and, without any sense of hope, set

out to save my life. I used to hate to hear things like, "What doesn't kill you, makes you stronger." I believe it now and it applies to the women who share here. Thank all of you. I also painted every room in my house and am good friends with a hand sander.

4. I find being allowed to hear yourself say, out loud, what you've gone through is so important. Especially when recovering from such a twisted 'reality.' A knowledgeable therapist to help guide your discovery, grief and healing process is invaluable. Learning about the disorder and participating in a support group can be life-affirming. I think having trusted friends who will allow you to talk about what you're experiencing until the tears turn to laughter is the most liberating part of the process. It's a long road and it's not something most people can relate to. Having to set boundaries of not being thought of as "the one who..." (<-insert tragedy here) and being allowed to grow past the victimization is a priceless gift that you can give to yourself. In time. Give yourself time.

5. Many things helped. For one, it is vitally necessary to know your own reality...no matter what is said to you. For me, writing my story has been enormously healing, and also reaching out to various politicians about my experiences in family court. Working towards change can help one to regain their sense of power. My case was the proverbial "straw that broke the camel's back" – and the final push that resulted in the termination of an inadequate Referee (essentially a Judge). Finally, I am focused most on keeping my eye on the big picture: mentally healthy kids and breaking the cycle of abuse.

Forgiveness

Divorce often brings forth images of fresh, crisp journal pages, in-depth soul searching, and the monumental pressure to forgive. We have been taught by virtually every religion under the sun that there is great power in forgiveness. Most studies on forgiveness tout the health benefits of forgiveness from both a mental and physical standpoint.

The art of forgiveness is simply letting go of hostility or resentment for a perceived transgression. The act of forgiveness is usually preceded by an admission of wrongdoing or an acknowledgement of the offense and, many times, a request for forgiveness. I had never struggled with forgiveness until I divorced a narcissist. A narcissist will never admit an indiscretion, nor are they capable of accepting responsibility, which leaves the offended party in an interesting predicament.

I believe that the key to forgiveness is that the offense in question is in the past. Anyone who has attempted to co-parent with a narcissist or other high-conflict personality knows that the past often repeats weekly and, in many cases, involves the children. I personally struggle with forgiveness as it directly relates to my ex-husband showing little or no regard for the well-being or safety of our children. When someone harms my child – whether it is emotionally or physically, the fierce momma bear comes forth and I am ready to protect. Forgiveness is not on my radar when the issues are constant, in the present tense, and involve harm to my children.

I have personally experienced the power of forgiveness, but not in the way that you may expect. I've spent a great deal of time sitting in therapy, penning my thoughts onto paper and digging deep to understand why I fell prey to a narcissist in the first place. I owned my role in the equation and I acknowledged the yellow, orange and red flags that I chose to ignore during our courtship. I then extended an olive branch and forgave myself. The healing that I experienced from forgiving myself was life-changing.

I recently spoke to Dr. Robert Enright, professor at the University of Wisconsin-Madison and founder of the International Forgiveness Institute, Inc. who eloquently weighed in on the topic of acceptance and forgiveness.

> *"To accept a person and to accept a situation are two different things. We can accept people who are unjust because they are mistaken, confused, and nonetheless possess inherent worth because they are persons. We should be careful in accepting unjust situations themselves, lest we grow complacent with the injustice. Accepting persons despite their flaws may be a marker on the path to forgiveness, which is difficult to accomplish in the short-run, especially when the injustices are on-going."*

While I have personally struggled with the topic of forgiveness, I have recently concluded that forgiveness is over-rated as it pertains to the narcissist. My personal resolution involves acceptance, rather than forgiveness. I am attempting to shift my perception of the situation by showing empathy for the personality disorder in general. What is life without loving and honest relationships with those around you? I accept that my ex-husband didn't choose to be narcissist. Acceptance of my ex-husband and my high-conflict divorce does not mean that I forgive his behavior or actions that continue to cause damage to our young children.

Advice from the Battlefield:

1. Forgive yourself for not knowing until you learned... Forgive yourself for not leaving before you did... Forgive the narcissist for being disordered when they didn't ask to be... Let the narcissist go, let "it" go, let yourself go... on and into your life. A life without the narcissist, without contact, without drama, without pain... if you can do that, in time, forgiveness will naturally occur... and just know that it does not require you to forget, just to forgive... Peace will come.

2. Forgiveness does not mean forgetting the abuse nor does it mean letting your guard down so that you are vulnerable to ongoing or future emotional abuse. Forgiveness means you let go of anger, resentment, anxiety, and depression that built up because of the narcissist's behaviors. What many people fail to realize is that forgiveness is a gift we give ourselves. We break the leash or tether between the narcissist and old hurts, which lightens our load and gives us peace and relief while we continue to place strong boundaries and limits with the narcissist to protect our current selves and our children.

3. It may not be easy, and I waivered back and forth on it, but I believe this says it best ....not forgiving is like drinking poison and expecting the other person to die. Forgiving is not saying what was done to you is okay or right. It is acknowledged and let go, because there is no other way not to be bitter or angry all the time. It's the only way to move forward, I think.

4. For me, it's a daily decision. Some days I feel like I can and have forgiven and other days... not so much. The good days are the days that I forgive myself for going through with a wedding when I knew there was something fundamentally wrong with him and with the whole relationship. When I forgive myself for giving my children the kind of cruel, selfish father that they will now have for the rest of their lives. When I forgive myself for not being stronger at times I know I should have been. When I forgive his parents for lying about who he really is to me and in court, and forgive him for being the way he is and causing the amount of pain he has. Other days I can't forgive. I can't even consider forgiving. I don't want to forgive. Those are the days that I see my kids hurting. My son crying uncontrollably in counseling that his father refuses to help pay for, knowing he wouldn't even need it if he didn't have the kind of father he has. Those are the hard days and the days I face all too often even now, 7 years post-divorce. Logically, I know that I need to forgive and not let him push my buttons but it is so hard when my heart hurts for my kids. I feel like I have caused their pain by choosing him.

5. Forgiveness is given when someone admits they have hurt you, which makes me feel that it is impossible for a narcissist to seek forgiveness or for myself to forgive a narcissist. They can't, and won't, admit it. They have believed their own lies for so long, it is who they are. I have to remind myself daily they are a narcissist and put them in their narcissist box. Different rules apply to these types of people. My biggest struggle is forgiving myself. I have failed in so many ways. I don't think I will ever be able to forgive myself for leaving without taking my children with me. The narcissist took this opportunity to teach them to hate me in just a few weeks. I allowed the narcissist to take everything away from me, leaving me an empty shell where once I was a fearless woman. I believe forgiveness takes a long time to achieve, but acceptance is the first step. Accepting our own choices and having determination to never end up where we were may bring self-forgiveness over time. I'm not there yet.

Going Public

I would love to be a fly on the wall of a divorce attorney's office. This profession is privy to the innermost details of a person's life and it probably takes a lot to make a divorce attorney cringe. In 2011, I did something that would make most divorce attorneys cringe: I began to openly and publicly blog about my divorce. I broke rule #108 of the divorce handbook: step away from the computer until the ink is dry on your divorce decree!

When I began my blog, "One Mom's Battle," I had no intention of anyone really *reading* my story. I wrote to purge myself from the chaos of my high-conflict divorce and to update my family and friends on the nightmare that I was living. As a person who runs screaming from conflict, I didn't understand what was happening to my life. I felt as though someone had strapped me to the front of a high speed train that had run off the tracks. If that wasn't scary enough, the train conductor was a mad man who took pleasure in watching the sheer terror in my eyes.

One year later, my blog has turned into an online support group for others around the world. While I never imagined that my blog would reach past my aunt in Chicago (love you, Aunt Bev!), I am grateful for the community of men and women who surround and inspire me daily.

I am often asked for my advice when it comes to publicly speaking about divorce battles. I am the first to admit that I walked into this world blindly and if I were able to rewind, I might do some things differently and possibly even use a pseudonym. Thankfully, my blog has not affected my case and my right to free speech has been upheld by the Commissioner presiding over our case. Sadly, I have heard situations where the writer was not as fortunate, and going public has gravely affected multiple custody battles that I am aware of. While I have been very careful to protect the identity of my ex-husband, truth be told and much to his dismay, this is not a story about him. My story is about divorcing a narcissist and the reader can insert the picture of the narcissist in their life because, sadly, my story is the same as Jane's in Oregon and Samantha's in Ireland.

While deciding whether to blog about your divorce, I recommend that you proceed with great caution when it comes to your children. I have installed K-9 parental controls on our home computers to block adult-related sites and my blog. If my daughters choose to read my blog as adults, there will be no surprises as, sadly, they have lived through this custody battle. My goal in writing is to educate those who have a hand in the Family Court System and to ensure that others feel less alone while divorcing a narcissist.

I recently reached out to an expert, Candace Smyth, Family Mediator, Attorney and Coach for her thoughts on taking divorce or child custody battles to the internet. Candace had some great advice to share and some items to ponder before you grab your keyboard and start typing:

> *"I would say that ideally everyone should talk to an attorney for advice about their particular scenario. Having said that, I would think about where energetically the inspiration for the blog is coming from. Is it coming from a place of wanting to make your ex pay for the pain he or she has caused you, or is it coming from a place of wanting to help others?*
>
> *Also, if considering writing about your divorce and you have children; really think about your children and how the writing could affect them. Are you bad-mouthing their other parent or speaking truth in a loving way knowing that you would share this with them anyway? If your kids are even older, just write it with the thought that they will read it. If younger, write it with the thought that they might one day read it.*
>
> *Now, from a more legal perspective, you just have to know that everything you put out there (just like with text messages and Facebook) is discoverable and can be used against you in the divorce proceedings. Knowing that, make the choice that is right for you and your family. There are some attorneys that would say "absolutely not, do not blog" when you are in any process of divorce or custody. If this is going to trigger even more anger in your spouse such that he or she will fight even harder in court for custody or financial division, then ask yourself if greater conflict is worth writing what you need to say. In the end, it is really up to you and depends on your situation.*
>
> *Some questions to ask yourself:*
>
> - *Will this increase conflict in the proceedings?*

- *Will my spouse or ex try to use what I write against me? Do I know he or she most likely will?*

- *Is my state a no-fault state or an at-fault state and is anything I am saying going to affect fault?*

- *Am I doing this from a solid, loving, honest place?*

- *Will the Judge assigned to my case consider this careless or disrespectful of the other parent such that it might affect custody?*

- *If so, and for all of these questions, is my mission here worth that risk?*

I think there is true value in honesty and transparency, but we have to be responsible in how we reveal personal stories. Especially when children are involved and a court is involved that has power to change things very quickly. As always, the more information you have, the more responsible decision you can make.

I never anticipated that my little online journal would reach the far corners of the world. Sometimes, I believe that there are plans in place that we don't understand and for that, I am also grateful. Journaling my story via my blog and book were the single-most healing things that I could have done. I kidded my therapist by saying that I found more peace writing my book than I did in three years of therapy. She is a *fantastic* therapist so that says a lot! Regardless of whether you decide to share your story publically, I highly recommend writing your story with pen and paper or a keyboard even if your mother is the only one who ever reads it. It is an incredibly healing experience.

Advice from the Battlefield:

1. I've started writing snippets of my story on the "One Mom's Battle: Australia" Facebook page and I find that it has been very cathartic for me to do so. However, I do keep in mind that the page is available to the public. I keep my words as neutral as possible, just in case my N-ex finds it. My custody battle, for the most part, is over. However I'm mindful that my words,

once in print, could be used against me. I stick to the facts and try and leave my emotions at the door.

2. I've been writing a private journal. At my most desperate moments I find that I can clarify my thinking by putting it down in writing. The next day I go back and check my writing for cohesive thought. It's a wonderful release to write it out. It's an affirmation of the journey to read it. I would strongly recommend that anyone journal. The story is there and needs to get out.

3. I journal privately. And just get it all go down on paper. I would recommend that you keep it private as often we have fears that can't be proven, and the narcissist's would love to use those against us.

4. I recall when I worked for CPS, a young gal had to turn over all her journals as part of the criminal trial against her father. Her private thoughts were no longer private. She was an emerging writer, and had been using the journals to help her heal. I used to write a lot, and know from my training how valuable that process can be not only in healing, but just in finding clarification to situations. I find myself not writing down my thoughts, or if I do, shredding them right away out of fear of having to turn over such a private part of me through discovery. It's painful to destroy them. I'm going through a modification right now and all emails, journals, letters, videos, etc. have been requested. Keeping silent, though, contributes to feelings of isolation.

5. I am so fortunate to have 3 amazing people in my life that have listened to every detail over the years. They understand how important it is to be able to share all of this stuff, and have provided my son and me with endless support. They were at both of my all-day hearings. Having them there gave me strength. I definitely talked and listened more than I wrote, but sometimes I would write an email to myself and vent...I always felt better after that.

I have always been delighted at the prospect of a new day, a fresh try, one more start, with perhaps a bit of magic waiting somewhere behind the morning. -J. B. Priestly

FAMILY COURT REFORM

The family court system in the United States is failing the children of our country. The court system is failing healthy, loving parents who are quickly stamped with titles like "alienator" or "over protective." Our appointed Judges and Commissioners are supposed to act in the best interests of the child, but unfortunately, they are not.

I am often invited to speak at events or join movements that are pro-mother and I politely decline every invitation. My own biological mother had the ability to procreate (obviously) however, that privilege did not (and should not) come with the ability to mentally or physically abuse a child. My mother suffered from mental illness along with drug and alcohol abuse yet, because she was a mother, she had rights. There are very few positive memories that I could share about my mother, yet the Family Court System awarded her visitation simply because she was my mother.

Something needs to change. Let's stop focusing on who has "rights" to a child and focus on what is truly best for the child. The pendulum has been swung too far in different directions when it comes to mothers' rights and fathers' rights. I am firmly against the notion that an individual should have rights just because they have the ability to procreate. A child's right to be safe and loved should supersede parental rights. When discussing Judges across the country, people are quick to tell me if the Judge is pro-mother or pro-father. This is a failure of our system. I yearn for the day when I start hearing that Judges are pro-children.

My case is classified as a "high-conflict divorce," however, the sad reality is that I went through a divorce with a person who thrives on conflict and does not care about the well-being of our children. Compared to drug abuse, physical abuse, sexual abuse and abandonment issues that are often addressed before us, my ex-husband, Seth, is a welcomed relief to the court. Seth seems educated, articulate and he is fighting for his children. Step back into reality for a moment and the truth is that Seth isn't fighting for custody of our children, he is fighting to win and to gain control. Winning and control are the primary driving forces of individuals with personality disorders.

I spoke to Bill Eddy, an attorney, therapist, and mediator and President of the High Conflict Institute. Mr. Eddy is on the frontlines of the crisis in the family courts and founded the "New Ways for Families" method of managing high-conflict family court cases. Mr. Eddy was kind enough to share the insight he has gained from being entrenched in the family court system:

> *"Tina Swithin is correct that the Family Court system is generally not educated about personality disorders, which creates several serious problems. Personality disorders are not obvious on the surface, which is why many people marry those with these disorders and why many courts are easily misled by them -- for months or years. To really understand what is going on takes looking under the surface and knowing what patterns of behavior to look for. This takes time and special knowledge, which family courts don't have, so decisions often favor those with the desperate emotions or the calculating control of those with personality disorders.*
>
> *The adversarial process of the court brings out the worst behavior for those with personality disorders. They become extremely defensive and often much more dangerous, as they resort to extreme efforts for power and control over the other party, the children, the professionals and the Judge. This can include lying, spreading rumors, hiding money, hiding children, false allegations and even violence. Many cases that I have read of family court-related shootings happen within 2-3 weeks of a court hearing.*
>
> *Family courts need more training, more time and more money for services for parents stuck in high-conflict cases. None of these are likely to occur any time soon -- in fact, the opposite is occurring. Yet society reaps what it sows and this is the future for many of the next generation. This is a mental health problem and a public health problem, and needs to be recognized as such."*

The Judges and commissioners of the family court system are too busy moving cases through the courtroom. It breaks my heart to think of the pain and suffering that children are going through due to an inept system. There needs to be on-going education about high-conflict divorces and personality disorders. Thankfully, there are people like Bill Eddy who are working tirelessly to provide education, but this is just the beginning of what is needed to make changes in our system.

Much like a doctor becomes accustomed to the cycle of life, our courts have become accustomed to abuse, neglect and abandonment. This issue begins in the courtroom and trickles down to everyone who has a hand in the family court system. This includes the very people who are supposed to protect our children, such as parenting evaluators, counselors and therapists, Guardians Ad Litem and Child Welfare Services. The family court system places a higher priority on parental rights than what is truly in the best interests of our children.

The following is a list of things that need to be changed in the Family Court System:

- **Words versus Actions**: When words and actions are not in alignment, further investigations should take place. Narcissists are master manipulators, yet their actions are never in alignment with their words.

- **Perjury**: Changes need to be made when it comes to individuals who are caught lying. Perjury is taken very seriously in every courtroom except the Family Court System. Why is this?

- **Education on Personality Disorders**: Education on NPD needs to begin in law school and continuing education on personality disorders should be mandatory for each person who has a hand in the Family Court System such as Custody Evaluators, Guardians Ad Litem, Commissioners, Judges, Social Workers and Attorneys.

- **The Best Interest of the Child:** Cases are often pushed through the courtroom like cattle. Ample time needs to be devoted to hearing high-conflict cases. When it takes longer to adopt a puppy from the dog pound than it does to decide the fate of a child, something is very wrong.

- **Court Orders:** Even with court orders in hand, it can be difficult to enforce those orders. When dealing with individuals with NPD, court orders need to be very concise and be devoid of wiggle room. If there is any room for manipulation in a court's orders, a narcissist will find it. All loopholes need to be closed.

- **Parental Rights versus Best Interests of the Child**: While the Family Court System is supposed to act in the best interests of the child, this is not happening. Parental rights seem to carry more weight than what is truly in the best interests of the child. The ability to procreate should not automatically guarantee rights that override a child's well-being.

While it takes a village to raise a child, it also takes a village to protect a child. The first step is to create a village within the Family Court System that is educated on personality disorders, as they are becoming increasingly prevalent in today's society. While I am thankful to Bill Eddy of the High Conflict Institute for the work he is doing to educate the courts, we need to ensure that this education is on-going and taking place in each and every courtroom across America.

Currently, my little grassroots village of "One Mom's Battle" is making changes by bringing awareness to this issue. As of February 2014, we have over one hundred Chapters of One Mom's Battle spread throughout five different countries. My village has grown from one mom to thousands of loving Warrior Parents – moms and dads united by one mission: to raise awareness on personality disorders in the Family Court System. It's going to take a huge village to make changes to this system. I encourage you to speak up, to write letters and to demand change.

"Never doubt that a small group of thoughtful, committed citizens can change the world; indeed, it's the only thing that ever has." -Margaret Mead

OMB STORIES OF HOPE

That was Then, This is Now

Tears welled up in my eyes as the new divorce decree and the enforcement order were entered into the court record. I could not believe that finally, after fifteen years of dealing with this narcissistic man, the tables had turned. I was overwhelmed with emotions ranging from relief to sadness to happiness.

I was married to Matt for eleven years, and we have two children. I knew within a few months of the wedding that I had married the wrong man. Looking back, there were red flags when we were dating, but I ignored them. Once married, I felt I had to make things work. We were Catholic and did not believe in divorce. My ex-husband is a successful engineer, and I am an administrator in a local school district. We should have been living the American dream, but my marriage was a nightmare.

At first, Matt and I fought a lot. He was never home, always at work. When he was home he could not be bothered with me. He watched TV in another room or talked to his brother on the phone for hours. Matt agreed to see a counselor and we went for a year. Things got a little better – when I learned to work around his moods. Matt became verbally abusive but only behind closed doors. He called me a "Fucking bitch" when he was mad, or he would get in my face and scream at me. He mocked me and tried to make me think I was paranoid or crazy. As I read this, it sounds insane that I put up with his behaviors. Why didn't I leave him? The abuse was gradual and happened over time; I did not realize how bad it had gotten. I was ashamed and embarrassed. I was the boss at work who helped others with their problems. How could this be happening to me?

Months and then years passed. Matt and I had two children, Cindy and Collin. Matt worked a lot, and the yelling and name-calling continued. I told myself that I could survive the bad marriage since he was never home. When the kids were little, I quit my job and worked part-time. I should have known then that we were in big trouble. Matt controlled everything. If I tried to spend money he would tell me that he made the money in the family. If I disciplined the kids, he would undermine me. If I cleaned up the garage, he would move the clutter back to its original spot. We were trying to pay off some debt and he decided we should forgo our debt to give money to his mom. It was as if the kids and I were an afterthought to him.

I joined a Mommy and Me group and made new friends. The kids and I
traveled and developed our own interests. Matt hated that Cindy, Collin, and
I were doing our own thing. When he came home from work after the kids
were in bed, he would wake them up. When he showed up on time, once
every two weeks, he would undermine my rules with the kids. He mimicked
me and made fun of me. He refused to cut the grass until it grew up to my
knees, but if I hired someone to cut it, he would scream and curse at me.
Again we went to counseling, but I came to realize that Matt did not want to
be with me. His anger got worse. He told me I was an embarrassment to him
and he did not want to be seen with me in public. Yet, in public, he acted like
he loved me. Once I had a group of friends over to scrapbook and he got in
my face and told me if I did not do what he said things were going to get ugly
for me. I was honest with my friends about the marriage, and the kids and I
fled to a friend's house to spend the night.

The final straw came one December afternoon. Matt, the kids, and I were
putting up Christmas decorations when Matt asked where I wanted to put the
tree. I suggested the middle of the living room and then changed my mind
and said the corner would be better. He started screaming at me that I was a
bitch and always changed my mind. As I stood there being berated, five-year-
old Cindy crawled under the kitchen table. She covered her ears with her
hands and said loudly, "I have to get out of here," over and over again.

That was the beginning of the end for me. For the first time in years, I had
clarity. I knew I had to get out, but I also knew Matt would go after me,
financially and emotionally. I KNEW he would try and take the kids from
me, so I got to work. I opened my own bank accounts and developed a
support network. I talked to my parents, my closest girlfriends, and my boss.
I found an attorney with a top law firm who was expensive, but I knew I
needed the best to protect myself and my kids. I prepared for a fight.

The divorce was very difficult for me. Matt filed for a jury trial and lied in
court documents saying I physically abused the kids, I had psychological
problems, and the kids wet their beds. He filed for full custody. I was beaten
down after being married to this man for so many years, but I knew I had to
fight. Matt tried to intimidate me by recording our conversations and taking
pictures of me constantly. Eventually, he was found in contempt of court, but

trumped up his own contempt charges against me. He emailed me constantly on Our Family Wizard telling me I was mentally ill. He brought his family and work colleagues to court to testify as to what a terrible mom I was. He did everything he could to ruin me, and what did I do? I settled with him. The divorce cost me almost $100,000.00 that I did not have. I was in debt and had to get away from him. The problem with settling is I made a deal with the devil. Matt's child support was reduced and he had custody of the kids ever day afterschool which gave him the opportunity to harass me. When he dropped the kids off he would yell at me and tell the kids how awful I was. He refused to send Cindy and Collin into the house when they came home. He would take pictures of me in my driveway and play in the cul de sac by himself in front of my house. He played ping pong at my next door neighbor's house. Once he parked on a nearby street with his car lights out and when I drove by, he followed me. I filed a police report on him for emailing me about having a gun. I tried to file a protective order, but since he had not physically harmed me, it was futile effort.

Once the divorce was final, Matt harassed me more, often stalking me. He followed me, called my house, drove by my house to see if I was home, and tried to sit near me at Cindy and Collin's games. He constantly glared at me at the kids' school functions and followed me to my car at the kids' practices. He told me he loved me and sent me emails about how he was still married to me in the eyes of the church. Finally, I had had enough. I was still paying off debt from the divorce but after two years of the harassment, I decided to get a new attorney and took Matt back to court to change the custody order and to increase child support to the standard amount. I discovered that my former attorney had "Undercharged" Matt and he owed me arrears in the amount of $13,000.00.

I had kept meticulous records that showed that Matt had violated the court order over 30 times since the divorce. Again he asked for a jury trial and full custody, trumping up contempt charges against me, and trying to prove me unfit. This time I was not afraid of him and I did not settle. The Judge lambasted Matt for stalking me and put harassment injunctions in the court order. Matt was found in contempt on three violations and had to pay $7,000 in attorney fees. He had to pay the arrearage, and child support was increased to the maximum amount. We did settle on one thing – the fact that I would decide extracurricular activities for the kids.

I know Matt will never take responsibility for his actions, but I am proud to have stood up to a dangerous bully. I showed him that if he chooses to harass and stalk me, there is a consequence. My job is to protect my children and myself. I do that, but it is too bad I have to protect us from the father of my children.

Blessed

Have you ever felt truly desperate? Not the habitual yearning for that first cup of coffee in the morning type of desperate. Or the too stressed out, must have a glass of wine (now!) type either.

I mean the soul crushing, bring you to your knees desperation when your life as you know it is crashing down around you. That which confirms you are merely an actor in the pathetic, sadistic existence that is your life. That desperation. Are you feeling me now?

I have felt this way twice in my life. Many times I was at the end of my rope, no place to turn, with no honest means of digging myself out of a particular situation. But twice, I have been on my knees, ready to throw in the towel. To give up. Accept my fate, as long as it was better than the hell penetrating my heart and every ounce of my being.

I was married to a sociopath. The scary type. The type of husband that leaves knots in your stomach morning, noon, and night. The one that makes your heart pound, your hands sweat, and leaves you shaking uncontrollably since you have no control over anything, least of all what he will do next. Everything you have ever known about yourself is now a huge ball of insecurity. You know the type. I'm certain you do.

The first time I ever felt truly desperate was the moment I realized my days were numbered. The instant I knew that if I did not escape that wretched excuse for a marriage, my life and my child's life would be over.

Maybe not right away. I had slowly been dying for years. Every day was more brutal than the one prior. But eventually, I was going to die in this marriage. I knew either he was going to kill me, or I was going to kill him. It had gotten that bad. After years of his threats, abuse, and addictions, he threatened to kill me. It was 4th of July weekend 2009. I remember it vividly.

In front of my child, in an extremely drunken rage, he manically screamed at me to, "Shut the fuck up, or I will shut you up forever." I believed him. I knew he was capable of it.

Guess what I did? I begged for help like my life, and my child's life, depended on it more than anything in my world ever had before.

That night after he had passed out stoned and drunk, and my child was asleep, I shut myself in my bathroom and crumbled into a heap on the bathroom floor.

I prayed like I never had before. I told God that I was empty. Hollow. Broken. And scared. Desperate! I had no idea how I had gotten so deep with a person who controlled every aspect of my existence. I had no idea how to fight for my life.

I asked God for help. I prayed with agonizing certainty that I would not survive if He didn't show Himself to me and make it absolutely clear what He wanted me to do. I would either end up dead, or I would end up in prison and leave my child motherless if I killed the SOB in a desperate attempt to protect myself and my child.

My mind began circling around me in a dark, swirling haze of fear, hate, and surrender. I was sobbing, yet had no tears. I was numb. I was dying. Inside and out, I was a shell of the person I had once been.

As soon as it began, it was over. I was calm. Scared to death, but calm. A booming voice in my head was telling me, "I am helping you."

The voice told me that no matter what the monster sleeping in the next room told me from that moment forward, I was not to believe it. If he told me again I was a worthless piece of shit, I was not to believe a word of it.

The voice filled my soul with love and hope. The love I felt in church as a child, that I knew came from a power greater than anything I could ever fathom. The unconditional love of my Maker.

He never left me. I turned away from Him during those dark years, but He never left my side. I knew it to be true. There was no mistaking it. I knew in that instant my child and I were going to be alright.

Fast forward ten months later. A lot happened in those ten months. I lost my father to heart disease. I left (finally!) the nightmare of the abusive marriage.

I saved my child and myself. I secured a little rental house for the two of us, the dog, and the cat. I successfully filed and received a domestic violence restraining order with the guidance of a women's' shelter. I filed for divorce, pro se.

I lived off my part time job without child or spousal support. I got groceries from the food bank at a local church. I had some utility bills paid by the graciousness of a local Catholic charity, just before our water and power were shut off. I borrowed some money from my brother and sister-in-law to make my car payment, which had fallen behind.

Soon after came the second feeling of utter desperation. I had gotten out. But I had no idea what to do. I had no money. Zilch. Just enough to pay the rent on our little house and put gas in my car.

How was I supposed to raise a child on my own with a part-time income? To put food on the table while fighting a high-conflict custody battle with a sociopathic, abusive addict? To stand victoriously on my own two feet, when I didn't even know where our next meal was coming from?

Again, I was on my knees. After I put my daughter to sleep that night, I crumbled on my bedroom floor. When desperate, when you feel like you have no clue how to go on, you crumble. Your legs fail. Your knees give out, and you're on the damn floor. Once again, I begged God to show me what in the world I was supposed to do to support myself and my child. I made a promise to God that night, one that He reminds me of daily when the small voice in my head reminds me where I came from. Where I've been. And where I'm going, come hell or high water.

I promised God that if He helped me—provided the answers I desperately needed—I would devote the rest of my lift to serving Him. Some way, somehow, I would dedicate my existence to living the life He intended for me. I pledged, in that desperate heap on my bedroom floor, if He saved my life (again!), that I would be faithful to Him until my dying day.

I dragged myself off the floor and fell asleep crying. I woke up with a clear head, and a clear heart. I could breathe. I felt—wait for it—almost happy. I felt free. I surrendered the fight and gave it to God. He was in charge now. Not me. He would see us through to the end. I didn't know how. I just knew it was true. *I had to pay attention to His signs, really listen, and trust when it was time for me to act.*

Fast forward a few months later. My company was advertising a position that was senior to that which I held at the time. I read the job description and knew I was qualified, albeit a long shot. It was located 250 miles away from where my child and I lived—from my hometown. I applied; what did I have to lose? After a series of interviews, I was selected over 60 other applicants, and offered a promotion.

I was awarded 100% sole legal and physical custody of my child and granted a move-away order in family court. I was going to support my little family on a salary three times what I was making. We moved. We struggled. We fought. We won. Desperate times call for desperate measures. Desperation brings us to our knees. This life we live is a blessing. It may feel like a living hell at times. In those moments, we have the ability to completely give up ourselves and surrender. Ask for help, receive it, and listen. I am blessed because I listened to the voice. I gave up control when it was obvious I had no control over anything. What a huge relief to be able to give the heavy burden to someone else! I let God guide my actions, my thoughts, and every move I made. It saved my life, and the life of my child. I am forever indebted to God's grace and mercy.

Peace

My daughter was completely snowed by the NNN, blindsided when he threw her out of the house, keeping the children. She complied when he said she was the problem and that she needed psychiatric help by going for psychological intake, etc. But with the help of her dad and I and other family friends, she snapped back to reality. She got her children back, faced the NNN and his attorney at first court hearing Pro Se, got an attorney appointed pro bono by Judge, started years of court issues trying to protect her babies that culminated with her getting sole physical and legal custody and supervised parenting time for NNN. She also found a non-narcissistic man who loves her and the kids and they have a happy life together. It was 4 years of drama, sometimes despair, but now they have peace as she puts one foot in front of the other. She did what she knew she needed to in order to protect her children.

Signs

My battle started in 2011 when the NNN changed the locks to a home that he
hadn't lived in for 3 months while I was at work. I got a restraining order,
took my children and left that home that I created and all that I "knew." The
NNN filed a bogus motion claiming I relocated the children wrongfully and
they had to be returned to the state that I left. They were with him for 30
days! During those days all I did was cry – and I did lose faith for a bit – but
then God gave me a sign. I continued to recall who was on the throne and
remained myself that I could do it and that I will! I moved back to the state
that I left, got an apartment with no money and no credit. I got 50/50 custody
of my children. I found this site shortly afterward and upon learning of NPD,
my life changed. No contact and documentation began. I familiarized myself
as much as I could with family law. I maintained a household and school fees
for 2 yrs without any support. In 2012 I was granted temporary sole custody
of my 2 children. While I am still in court (I go back tomorrow), when I look
back on what I have been through with the NNN and lean on all that I have
learned through my battle, I know that the hard days will be a thing of the
past and that we will get through it.

OMB

I am impatiently waiting my trial date (2 years in the making). In the
beginning, adjournment after adjournment was extremely frustrating. We
became homeless. Everything that could go wrong, did go wrong. At that
point, I was ready to give up. He had all the control and I felt that I just
couldn't win. His mistress is a bigger Narcissist than him and the two against
one was too much for me. Then I found Tina's blog. I was in shock. I could
not believe someone else out there had been living my life. I couldn't stop
reading. This gave me the hope and strength I needed to get back up and
fight. During this time, learning about NPD, hearing so many stories that
could be my own, there were failed mediations, arguments with the Narcs but
I still felt like I could do it. If we had not had all those adjournments, NNN's
attorney would have torn me apart. I would have gone into that courtroom
full of emotion expecting the courts to rule fairly and just. They most likely
wouldn't have. You see, I am now grateful for having all this time to educate
myself about NPD, and the family courts. It has also given time for NNN to
show his true colors, and he just keeps showing them as more time passes. I
am ready now. I know how it works where I didn't before. So when we think
we really want something and don't get it, often there is a reason we don't see

at the moment. I still don't know how it will turn out, but I do know that I'm prepared and fighting back with all I've got!

No Contact

First of all, I know my story isn't over but it has definitely turned around and gotten better! A very, very long story short....my N-ex abused me in more ways than I care to recount and during the final months I also had a miscarriage (we have 1 child together)....afterwards I had the strength to leave but the abuse continued and I ended up having a breakdown for 10 minutes one day......those 10 minutes have been used against me for years now to try and prove I'm unstable. At first he was successful in gaining full custody of our daughter....who, to make matters more complicated, is disabled. He denies her issues and proper care for her at every opportunity because his ego can't stand the fact that his child is disabled. Anyway it took over 2 1/2 years (during mostly to his repeated continuances and other forms of stalling) but I went from visitation to 50% custody.....then last year I gained full custody with no contact or visits for him (sadly this happened because my daughter reported abuse to her teacher). He continues to try to regain custody.....and of course he wants unsupervised, full physical (typical N), but he has not gotten it. It was recently ordered for them to attend reunification therapy. We will see what happens, but my daughter has been having the best school year she has ever had since starting kindergarten. Hopefully things will continue to go well for her! I am strong enough to deal with his nonsense now.....it's just my daughter I worry about....her and the 3 innocent children his new naive wife has now brought into this world. It's the 4 of them I continue to pray for!

Marathon

Four years ago, super-wealthy husband bought a house in another state without my knowledge. He cleaned out all of our bank accounts and took off with our 3-year-old son. I was a SAHM left with no resources. You know the story! Our first Judge died one day after our initial hearing, leaving us with NO court opportunities for 6 months. I was diagnosed in a court ordered psych evaluation as depressed, combative, and non-functioning. Amazingly lucky to have an attorney who basically worked for free, saying she would get the money at some point from him. We also had a guardian, which he requested, who saw through him. A former work colleague gave me a high level corporate job in a horrible recession, despite my having not worked in 8 years. And a Judge who got it. As you know, this is a marathon, not a sprint. It has taken 4 years. I now have full legal and physical custody of our son. My ex-husband has been ordered to pay all my attorney's fees, he has to pay for private school, and he finally has to pay child support and back child support. Initially, he paid through garnished wages and now he pays voluntarily on his own. He has our case now in our state supreme court, but just last week the court denied his request to halt the mandate of our decision. So, in a few weeks, I will also be able to collect my marital settlement from funds that had been frozen. I read the stories on "One Mom's Battle" and realize just how lucky I am. It can happen! Stay strong, ladies, and stay the course!

Mama Bear

I filed for divorce in the summer of 2011 (domestic violence and all the other NNN marital traits one can have). At the time I had no idea ex was a Narcissist and I thought he had the best intentions for our kids. After leaving, he hurt our son. Our daughter was hurt in his care (reports filed by the kids' pediatricians, nothing done by child services), and the stalking started. I had a breakdown and he slandered me throughout our community – when I finally got a restraining order protecting myself and my kids, he turned around and got people to lie about me. As a result, the kids were taken from me. (I had a stress psychosis, there is major child abuse in my history as well) I lost my kids for 5 months but I do believe everything happens for a reason (even if it doesn't make sense at the time). I was blessed to have an amazing attorney take my case (and he continued to work for me even when my money ran out) and a therapist who understood trauma, PTSD, narcissism and taught me how to deal with all the attacks that I was under. Including that my exN was trying to break me. I went through dark days, days I never knew existed, and learned that the court system is not about justice or protecting children. Most importantly, I learned the strength of a mama bear. And I never gave up. I have had my kids back for 1.5 years. They live with me 70% of the time now, and I continue to recover and heal. And in the end, the best revenge is "a happy life." It just takes time. And one thing about NNN's: just stand out of their way and give 'em more rope because their true colors do finally come through. Sending peace, love and hope to all you beautiful mamas (and papas) who have unfairly lost your children. I never, ever thought I would lose my children... but don't give up hope. Sending peace, love and light.

True Colors

After years of costly litigation I had no choice but to go Pro Se in the middle of a trial. At the time, I felt this was the worst thing to happen to me. My attorney was grateful that I admitted that I would not be able to pay his fee at the end of trial, and by that point had seeing my ex-husband's narcissistic tendencies. Not only did he offered to reduce my final bill, but he also to assist me for free with filing paperwork and formulating questions free of charge. When faced with questions in court from me, the person he should control, my ex was unable to control his anger and rage. It was then that I realized that going Pro Se, something I thought was the worst thing possible, was actually working to my benefit. For, had it been my lawyer cross examining him, my ex would have been able to continue to hide his true colors. I am convinced that everything happens for a reason -- and this is just one more example! Plus, with the financial burden lifted, litigation was actually LESS stressful.

"Hope is like a road in the country; there was never a road, but when many people walk on it, the road comes into existence." **-Lin Yutang**

<u>RESOURCES</u>

Education on this disorder is imperative. Recent statistics show that up to 16% of college students show traits of Narcissistic Personality Disorder. After three years of advocacy work in this field, I am thoroughly convinced that everyone is a potential target for these individuals, regardless of education or social status. Over the past few years, I have met some of the most brilliant people who share one common thread: they have all fallen victim to someone with Narcissistic Personality Disorders. No one is immune from NPD: not attorneys, medical professionals, psychologists or professors.

Whether you are divorcing a narcissist or work with someone who is a narcissist, education is power. Education is the key to flipping the switch from victim to survivor. If you are ready to flip the switch, here are some resources to help you on your journey.

Books

- **Divorcing a Narcissist: One Mom's Battle**- Tina Swithin
- **Why Does He Do That?- Inside the Minds of Angry and Controlling Men**- Lundy Bancroft
- **When Dad Hurts Mom**- Lundy Bancroft
- **Will I Ever Be Good Enough? Healing the Daughters of Narcissistic Mothers**- Karyl McBride
- **Safe People: How to Find Relationships That Are Good for You and Avoid Those That Aren't**- Henry Cloud and John Townsend
- **Boundaries: When to Say Yes, How to Say No to Take Control of Your Life**- Henry Cloud and John Townsend
- **Divorce Poison**- Dr. Richard A. Warshak
- **Stop Walking on Eggshells**- Paul Mason MS and Randi Kreger
- **Splitting: Protecting Yourself While Divorcing Someone with Borderline or Narcissistic Personality Disorder**- Bill Eddy LCSW JD and Randi Kreger
- **BIFF: Quick Responses to High Conflict People**- Bill Eddy LCSW JD
- **Invisible Heroes: Survivors of Trauma and How They Heal**- Belleruth Naperstek

- **Ditch that Jerk: Dealing with Men who Control and Hurt Women**- Pamela Jayne

- **The Sociopath Next Door**- Martha Stout

- **Escaping the Boy: My Life with a Sociopath**- Paula Carrasquillo

- **The Verbally Abusive Relationship**- Patricia Evans

- **Trauma Proofing Your Kids**- Peter Levine and Ph.D. and Maggie Kline

- **Rethinking Narcissism: the Bad—and Surprising Good—About Feeling Special**- Dr. Craig Malkin

- **Born for Love**- Bruce D. Perry

Websites, Blogs and Forums

- **One Mom's Battle** (Tina Swithin)

- **The Lemonade Club** (Tina Swithin's Private Forum)

- **After Narcissistic Abuse There is Light, Life and Love** (Facebook Page)

- **The Perils of Divorced Pauline** (Pauline)

- **Safe Relationships** (Sandra L. Brown, MA)

- **Love Fraud** (Donna Anderson)

"Education is not the filling of a pail,

but the lighting of a fire." -William Butler Yeats

<u>GRATITUDE</u>